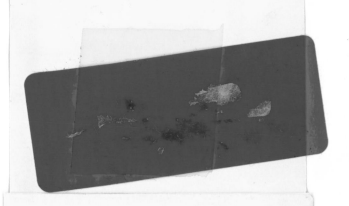

SHAKESPEARE'S TRAGEDIES

Literature and Life series
(Formerly Modern Literature and World Dramatists)
General Editor: Philip Winsor

Complete list of titles in the series on request.

Shakespeare's
TRAGEDIES

PHYLLIS RACKIN

WITH HALFTONE ILLUSTRATIONS

FREDERICK UNGAR PUBLISHING CO.

NEW YORK

Copyright © 1978 by Frederick Ungar Publishing Co.,
Inc.
Printed in the United States of America
Designed by Edith Fowler

Library of Congress Cataloging in Publication Data
Rackin, Phyllis.
  Shakespeare's tragedies.

  (World dramatists)
  Bibliography: p.
  Includes index.
  1. Shakespeare, William 1564–1616—Tragedies.
l. Title.
PR2983.R27   822.3'3   75-34216
ISBN 0-8044-2706-2 cloth
ISBN 0-8044-6668-8 paper

Third Printing,

For Rebecca Jane Rackin,
who spent all those beautiful bright summer
days minding her little sister.

CONTENTS

CHRONOLOGY

1564   William Shakespeare is born in Stratford-upon-Avon. The church register records his baptism April 26; but there is no record of his birth, which is usually celebrated on April 23, the day of England's patron Saint George as well as the anniversary of Shakespeare's death. His father, John Shakespeare, is a glover and his mother, Mary Arden, the daughter of a prosperous farmer.

1568   John Shakespeare is elected Bailiff (equivalent to mayor) of Stratford. Now a prosperous businessman, the owner of several houses and the holder of public offices, he applies to the College of Heralds for the right to a coat of arms. In the 1570s and 1580s, however, his fortunes decline; he falls into debt and is removed from his post as alderman for failure to attend Stratford Council meetings.

1582   A license is issued on November 27 for the marriage of William Shakespeare and Anne Hathaway.

1583   Shakespeare's daughter Susanna is christened on May 26.

1585 Shakespeare's twin son and daughter, Hamnet and Judith, are christened on February 2.

1592 Philip Henslowe, manager of the Rose Theatre, records in his diary for March 3 the performance of a new play, "harey the vj" (probably written around 1590).

In September Robert Greene, in his *Groatsworth of Wit*, attacks an "vpstart Crow, beautified with our feathers, that with his *Tygers hart wrapt in a Players hyde*, supposes he is as well able to bombast out a blanke verse as the best of you and ... is in his owne conceit the onely Shake-scene in a countrey." (Compare, in *3 Henry VI*, I, iv, "O tiger's heart wrapped in a woman's hide!")[1] Although the exact date when Shakespeare arrives in London is unknown, Henslowe's note and Greene's attack show that by 1592 he is already established there as an actor and has had at least one of his plays produced. From 1592 to 1594 his career is probably interrupted by severe outbreaks of the plague, which repeatedly closed the London theaters.

1593 Shakespeare's poem *Venus and Adonis* is published. *The Comedy of Errors, Richard III, Titus Andronicus*, and *The Taming of the Shrew* are probably written about this time.

1594 Shakespeare's poem *The Rape of Lucrece* is published. *The Two Gentlemen of Verona, Love's Labour's Lost*, and *King John* are often dated this year.

A record of a payment to William Kempe, William Shakespeare, and Richard Burbage, "seruantes to the Lord Chamberleyne," for Court performances on December 26 and 27 shows that Shakespeare is now a sharer in one of London's two major acting companies.

1595   *Romeo and Juliet, Richard II,* and *A Mid-summer-Night's Dream* are probably written about this time.

1596   John Shakespeare is granted the right to a coat of arms.

The Merchant of Venice is often assigned to this year.

Shakespeare's son, Hamnet, is buried in Stratford on August 11.

1597   William Shakespeare buys New Place, one of the two largest houses in Stratford.

The two parts of *Henry IV* are generally dated 1597–98.

1598   Francis Meres publishes his *Palladis Tamia*, which praises Shakespeare for "his *Gentlemen of Verona,* his *Errors,* his *Loue labors lost,* his *Loue labours wonne,* his *Midsummers night dreame,* & his *Merchant of Venice* ... his *Richard the 2. Richard the 3. Henry the 4.,* King *Iohn, Titus Andronicus* and his *Romeo and Iuliet*" as well as "his *Venus and Adonis,* his *Lucrece,* his sugred Sonnets among his priuate friends, &c." The identity of *Loue labours wonne* has been the subject of much scholarly debate.

1599   The Globe Theatre is built; William Shakespeare is one of the original investors, with a one-tenth share. *Much Ado about Nothing* and *Henry V* are usually dated 1598 or 1599; and *Julius Caesar, As You Like It, Twelfth Night* and *The Merry Wives of Windsor,* 1599 or 1600.

1601   The Earl of Essex's followers sponsor a performance of *Richard II* at the Globe on the afternoon of February 7, before their abortive rebellion against Queen Elizabeth.

On September 8 John Shakespeare is buried in Stratford.

The probable year of *Hamlet* is 1601.

1602 This is the probable year of *Troilus and Cressida* and the possible year of *All's Well That Ends Well*, although its date is problematical.

1603 Queen Elizabeth dies on March 24. James VI of Scotland is crowned James I of England.

A severe outbreak of plague closes the theaters. Shakespeare's company, the Lord Chamberlain's Men, becomes the King's Men.

1604 The theaters reopen in April.

Measure for Measure and *Othello* are usually dated 1604.

1605 *King Lear* and *Macbeth* are usually dated 1605.

1607 On June 5 Shakespeare's daughter Susanna marries John Hall in Stratford.

Antony and Cleopatra is probably written in 1606 or 1607, and *Coriolanus* is often dated 1607 or 1608. *Timon of Athens* is sometimes assigned to 1607, but estimates vary widely.

1608 Shakespeare's granddaughter Elizabeth is christened on February 21.

Shakespeare's company leases the Blackfriars Theatre on August 9. Shakespeare held a one-seventh share.

On September 9 Shakespeare's mother is buried in Stratford.

Pericles, first published in 1609, is often dated 1608.

1609 Shakespeare's sonnets are published by Thomas Thorpe. Meres mentioned the sonnets in 1598, but their exact date and the order of their composition are unknown, although most of them were probably composed in the mid 1590s. *Cymbeline* is probably written this year.

1610 *The Winter's Tale* is probably written this year.

1611 *The Tempest*, performed at court on November 1, is probably written in 1611.

1612 Shakespeare's deposition in Stephen Belott's lawsuit against Christopher Mountjoy (May 11) suggests that by this time he had retired to Stratford, for he is identified as "William Shakespeare of Stratford vpon Aven in the Countye of Warwicke."

1613 On June 29 the Globe Theatre burns down during a performance of *Henry VIII* (probably written in 1612 or 1613).

1616 Judith Shakespeare marries Thomas Quiney on February 10.
William Shakespeare dies in Stratford on April 23.

1623 Shakespeare's fellow actors John Heminge and Henry Condell publish the First Folio, the first collected edition of his plays. The Folio, which is the first text we have for a number of the plays, divides the plays into comedies, tragedies, and histories, but it does not give them in order of composition. Scholars therefore have attempted to establish their dates from various evidence—records of performances, contemporary references, dates of the quartos, entries in the Stationers' Register, allusions within the plays to contemporary events, and other, more subjective criteria, like the quality of the blank verse and language. In many cases, therefore, the dates of the plays are subject to dispute; the ones given here represent the current scholarly consensus.

A PERSONAL ENCOUNTER

The study of Shakespeare's plays can become a lifetime vocation. Books and essays on Shakespeare, studies erudite and obsessed, profound and trivial, can (and do) fill libraries. And there is no end in sight. The sheer mass of accumulated commentary is likely to bewilder a beginning student with the unspoken message that Shakespeare is a Serious Classic, accessible to learned specialists only. But it is worth remembering that William Shakespeare was a popular playwright long before he became an Institution, and that even today he is probably the most popular playwright in the world.

Shakespeare was not the most learned playwright in Elizabethan England, but he made money from his plays because all kinds of people, ignorant as well as learned, wanted to see them. In our own time, Shakespeare's plays still fill London theaters, and theaters from Paris to Tokyo as well. Shakespeare festivals are held in every region of the United States, from Alabama to Utah, from Texas to Vermont. The plays still attract large and varied audiences.

Some members of this immense modern audience undoubtedly go to do their pious duty to the cultural monument that Shakespeare has become; some, no doubt, are professional Shakespeareans attending a performance as part of their work. But scholars and pious pilgrims alone could not fill all these theaters. Most of the people in the audience are what they were in Shakespeare's own time—simply amateurs (that is, lovers) of the plays they have come to see.

This book is written for amateurs. Some of the chapters incorporate material I have published in scholarly journals, and others include original material not published elsewhere. But my main purpose is to make more and better amateurs—to help readers come into contact with Shakespeare's tragedies, not as pious worshipers and not as learned scholars, but simply as human beings, using their own intelligence and sensitivity to discover the human significance that has earned these plays their place at the very center of our cultural tradition.

I include a chapter on stage history because Shakespeare's plays were written for a particular theater, and a good reading should include an effort to imagine the play as it may have been performed on Shakespeare's stage. The chapters on the individual tragedies are designed to be read in conjunction with the texts of the plays. None of them can stand alone as a picture— or even a map—of the play's terrain. They are more like signs, pointing to roads that readers must take for themselves. I pay close attention to language, because Shakespeare's tragedies are poetry as well as drama. I explain some of the ideas and dramatic conventions that were familiar in Shakespeare's time but unfamiliar today, and I mention some of the issues that have perplexed scholars and provoked debate. But my chief concern throughout is to help readers make contact with the plays.

Because Shakespeare's tragedies approximate life itself in richness and variety, the ways of approaching them are legion. For each play, I indicate only one or two angles of approach. In the case of *Romeo and Juliet* and *Macbeth*, for instance, I emphasize symbolic language; in *Hamlet*, plot; in *Othello*, character; in *Antony and Cleopatra*, theatrical strategy. None of my essays aspires to be comprehensive, but taken together they do indicate a variety of ways to approach Shakespeare's tragedies. For each play, I focus on questions that should lead readers fairly directly to central issues in that particular work, but all of these approaches can be applied productively to any of the plays.

Although I am convinced of the merit of my approaches, I do not insist upon the value of my interpretations. All critical interpretations (including my own) should be approached warily. Fidelity to the text is an essential criterion: an interpretation that cannot be supported by evidence from the text and projected in the theater is likely to be an expression of the interpreter's beliefs rather than a valid statement about Shakespeare's play. On the other hand, a text may support numerous interpretations, and theories that seem to preclude each other can often be reconciled as complementary aspects of a richer, more inclusive, and therefore more revealing view of the play.

Shakespeare's tragedies have retained their central place in our literature for almost four hundred years because successive generations have continued to find in them reflections of their own predicaments and expressions of their own deepest concerns. In every age, critics and readers, actors and directors, have reinterpreted the plays in terms of their own experience. Sometimes older interpretations have been found wrong, but more often the plays have simply revealed new dimensions of their meanings as succeeding generations have brought new concerns to the theater or the text.

The study of Shakespeare commentary is itself an

exciting subject, telling us much about the intellectual history of our civilization from the late Renaissance to the present. But the study of Shakespeare's plays demands more than erudition. Criticism and scholarship can only help us to discover the text, can only indicate ways to approach the life embodied there. The actual discovery requires a personal encounter.

THE TRAGEDIES

Titus Andronicus

Titus Andronicus is the earliest of Shakespeare's tragedies we have, and the least successful. First printed in 1594, it may have been written much earlier. This crudely sensational play seemed outmoded even within Shakespeare's lifetime; in 1614 Ben Jonson derided its admirers as men whose judgment "hath stood still these five-and-twenty or thirty years." It has not been frequently performed, and some scholars have tried to demonstrate that a work so obviously inferior must have been written by someone other than Shakespeare.

All the evidence we have, however, indicates that Shakespeare did write *Titus Andronicus*. Francis Meres included it in his list of Shakespeare's plays in *Palladis Tamia*, three quarto editions were printed during Shakespeare's lifetime, and Shakespeare's fellow actors included it in the First Folio. Moreover, *Titus Andronicus* anticipated Shakespeare's great tragedies in a number of ways that provide useful indications of his evolution from the maker of a typical Elizabethan revenge tragedy to the great artist who was to transform the stale conventions he inherited.

The plot of *Titus Andronicus* is neatly mechanical,

perfectly obedient to the five-part scheme the Elizabethans had inherited from the Greeks and Romans, and the action is packed with the sensational episodes that were the Elizabethans' own specialty. Of the twenty-two characters in *Titus Andronicus*, fourteen are dead by the end of the play, and most of the killing takes place on stage. In the last act there are three on-stage killings within four lines, as well as a number of others, spaced at more reasonable intervals. A feast of human flesh takes place before the audience, as does the butchery of the characters who will be its ingredients, and Titus carefully describes his grisly plans to his victims before he kills them:

> Hark, villains! I will grind your bones to dust,
> And with your blood and it I'll make a paste;
> And of the paste a coffin [that is, piecrust] I
>   will rear
> And make two pasties of your shameful
>   heads,
> And bid that strumpet, your unhallowed dam,
> Like to the earth swallow her own increase.
> This is the feast that I have bid her to,
> And this the banquet she shall surfeit on.
>   (V, ii)

Although Elizabethan productions were not generally realistic, the audiences apparently liked scenes of violence and bloodshed, and the actors devoted considerable ingenuity to staging such spectacles. *Titus Andronicus* is an extraordinarily gory play, even within this bloody and sensational tradition, but the accumulation of horrors in it remains curiously unimpressive. The play's failure cannot be attributed simply to its bloodiness, for Shakespeare never really abandoned the tradition of blood and violence, even in his mature tragedies. *Macbeth* is steeped in blood, in action as well as imagery. At the end of *Hamlet* the stage is just as thickly strewn with corpses as it is at the end of *Titus Andronicus*. And in *King Lear* Shakespeare included the dreadful scene of Gloucester's blinding, certainly as horrifying as the disgusting banquet in *Titus Andronicus*. But *Titus Andronicus* is all surface and sensationalism; and for all its anticipations of Shakespeare's great tragedies, it remains an inferior play. The blood that flows so freely from the first scene to the last is, as one critic wittily observed, merely "ornamental." The horrors have no serious thematic or psychological point. The characterization is thin and stereotyped, so that the exaggerated sufferings of the characters fail to move us, and the dialogue is unrealistic and stiff.

Consider, for instance, the following passage, in which the evil Aaron greets his equally villainous mistress Tamora in the woods outside Rome:

> Madam, though Venus govern your desires,
> Saturn is dominator over mine.
> What signifies my deadly-standing eye,
> My silence and my cloudy melancholy,
> My fleece of woolly hair that now uncurls,
> Even as an adder when she doth unroll
> To do some fatal execution?
> No, madam, these are no venereal signs.
> Vengeance is in my heart, death in my hand,
> Blood and revenge are hammering in my head.
>
> (II, iii)

Aaron does not express his feelings; he describes them. The verse form—stiffly regular, end-stopped iambic pentameter—contributes to the artificiality of the dialogue, as does the imagery, which tends to be classical or conventionally "dreadful" and almost never freshly observed or unpretentious.

Titus Andronicus is usually studied as an example of Shakespeare's early style or of the crude neo-

Senecan tragedy so popular on the English stage when he began writing. The Latin plays attributed to Seneca, widely studied, translated, and imitated during the Renaissance, were marked by strict plot structure, sensational events (Seneca's *Thyestes* anticipates the banquet of human flesh in *Titus Andronicus*), a revenge theme, ghosts, a bloody denouement, high-born characters, an elevated style, stichomythia, sententious rhetoric, and long speeches of narrative or of stoic meditation on the fickleness of fortune, the fleetingness of life, and the mutability of all things. To these ingredients, the Elizabethans added embellishments—madness, real or pretended (*Titus Andronicus*, like *Hamlet*, has both), and the display of atrocities on stage (Seneca and his more academic imitators had them reported by a messenger). The sensational and moralistic elements had obvious appeal, and the basic Senecan theme of a fall from great prosperity to the depths of adversity was also congenial to the Elizabethans, for it fit the notion of tragedy they had inherited from the Middle Ages as a fall from high estate, a descent on the wheel of fortune, reminding Christians of the vanity of all worldly glory.

Although the total effect of *Titus Andronicus* is more sensational than instructive, all its ingredients follow the standard neo-Senecan recipe, and the villain Aaron comes from the equally familiar tradition of the "Machiavel." Crudely modeled on a vulgarized popular image of the Italian political philosopher Niccolò Machiavelli, the Machiavel in Elizabethan drama was a self-confessed villain, characterized by cynicism, opportunism, atheism, treachery, self-centeredness, and a wholehearted dedication to evil for its own sake. The Machiavellian villain, unlike such sinners as Macbeth and Claudius, is not driven to crime by a compelling passion or ambition. Instead, he takes an artistic delight in his wicked work, relishing the very process of crime rather than simply looking forward to the benefits it will win him. At the end of *Titus Andronicus*, Aaron, having been caught, gleefully confesses. Asked, "Art thou not sorry for these heinous deeds?" he replies, in orthodox Machiavellian fashion:

> Ay, that I had not done a thousand more.
> Even now I curse the day—and yet, I think
> Few come within the compass of my curse—
> Wherein I did not some notorious ill,
> As kill a man, or else devise his death,
> Ravish a maid, or plot the way to do it,
> Accuse some innocent and forswear myself,
> Set deadly enmity between two friends,
> Make poor men's cattle break their necks,
> Set fire on barns and hay-stacks in the night,
> And bid the owners quench them with their
>   tears.
> Oft have I digg'd up dead men from their
>   graves
> And set them upright at their dear friends'
>   door,
> Even when their sorrow almost was forgot;
> And on their skins, as on the bark of trees,
> Have with my knife carved in Roman letters,
> "Let not your sorrow die, though I am dead."
> Tut, I have done a thousand dreadful things
> As willingly as one would kill a fly,
> And nothing grieves me heartily indeed
> But that I cannot do ten thousand more.
>   (V, i)

At this point in the play, the audience is likely to be heartily glad he cannot—not because they are horrified at the villainy but because they are bored with the horrors.

Some scholars have argued that *Titus Andronicus* is not an imitation but a parody of the bloody revenge tragedies, and a few modern critics and directors have

seen in its senseless accumulation of horrors an anticipation of our own theater of the absurd. But parody or
not, the play still seems curiously deficient. Although
the hero and his enemies are highly illustrious and
hold the highest offices in the state, the state itself does
not achieve the cosmic significance it has in Shakespeare's later tragedies. It is not a metaphor for the
universe; indeed, we do not value it any more than we
do the characters. In the long run *Titus Andronicus*
seems destined to remain what it has been considered
by most critics since the time it was written—a
singularly faulty (and perhaps therefore singularly
instructive) product of a playwright who was never
again to write so badly.

Romeo and Juliet

To many critics, the effect of *Romeo and Juliet* is not tragic but pathetic. The lovers, they argue, are not the agents of their fate but only victims. They lack heroic stature, their helplessness elicits pity but no fear or exaltation, their undoing illustrates no universal law of retribution, and their struggles give us no heroic defiance of human limitation to admire. In short, their story lacks tragic stature, for it implies an immature view of the human condition—that nothing is our fault or responsibility and that fate, like a tyrannical or capricious parent, will deprive us of happiness for no explicable reason.

The play offers considerable evidence to support this view. Chance, the typical agent of malevolent fate in a deterministic universe, plays a major role in the plot. Romeo meets Juliet by chance; he meets Tybalt and Mercutio by chance when they are fighting; chance keeps Friar John from delivering Friar Laurence's message to Romeo; and the entire scene in the Capulet tomb depends upon chance and bad timing for its outcome.

What chance does not accomplish in causing the lovers' ruin, other characters do. Tybalt's murder of

Mercutio, which reawakens the dormant feud between the Montagues and the Capulets, is not only not
Romeo's fault; it is an act he tries to prevent. Similarly,
old Capulet seems as capricious as fate itself, and as
impervious to the lovers' wishes, when he suddenly
decides to move up the date of Juliet's wedding to
Paris.

Although the plot depends upon chance and coinci-
dence, Shakespeare makes the outcome seem inevitable
by loading the play with foreshadowings and premonitions of doom. In theology the relationship between God's foreknowledge and our predestination has
been debated for centuries, but in literature the audience's foreknowledge necessarily implies the characters'
predestination—psychologically even if not logically.
What the audience knows will happen must happen,
and before any of the characters comes on stage, the
Prologue announces that the lovers will be "star-
cross'd," their love "mark'd" by "death." The lovers'
own premonitions of their fate maintain our sense of its
inevitability as the play progresses. Before Romeo goes
to the Capulets' party, at which he will meet Juliet
for the first time, he says he fears that "Some conse-
quence yet hanging in the stars/Shall bitterly begin his
fearful date/With this night's revels, and expire the
term" of his life "By some vile forfeit of untimely
death" (I, iv). As soon as Romeo declares his love,
Juliet says, "Although I joy in thee,/I have no joy of
this contract to-night;/It is too rash, too unadvis'd, too
sudden,/Too like the lightning, which doth cease to
be/Ere one can say it lightens" (II, ii). These are the
first of many such instances.

Like the foreshadowing, the dramatic irony in the
play emphasizes the lovers' helplessness, for every instance reminds the audience that its knowledge is
superior to the lovers'. Perhaps the most poignant
example occurs when Romeo sees Juliet sleeping in the

tomb, apparently dead: he marvels that she still looks alive, but, ironically, he drinks the fatal potion anyway.

Shakespeare further intensifies our sense of the lovers' helplessness by alterations he made in his source material. Juliet's age in previous versions was eighteen or sixteen, but in Shakespeare's play she is not yet fourteen. Shakespeare also devotes much of the first act to establishing Romeo's adolescent infatuation for Rosaline. Shakespeare reduced the time of the action from nine months to five days; and whether or not the play was actually performed, as the Prologue suggests it was, in only two hours, it does seem to rush before our eyes in a whirlwind of events over which the lovers have no control.

There are, to be sure, some indications that the lovers are agents of their fate as well as its victims. The family feud lies more or less dormant until Romeo kills Tybalt. It is first presented in the play as a comic brawl between serving men. When old Capulet calls for a sword to join the fray, his wife responds (I, i), "A crutch, a crutch! why call you for a sword?" and Lady Montague physically restrains her own husband from joining in. When the Prince orders the feuding families to keep the peace, both Montague and Capulet are willing to obey; Capulet says (I, ii), " 'tis not hard, I think,/For men so old as we to keep the peace." When Romeo describes his unrequited love for Rosaline, he never mentions the feud as an impediment, even though she is Capulet's niece. When Tybalt storms because Romeo, a Montague, has come to the Capulet party, the old man responds by speaking well of Romeo's bearing and reputation and warning Tybalt to mind his manners lest he spoil the party. This evidence that the old feud is not all that serious when the play opens suggests that Romeo is more agent than victim.

Nevertheless, Romeo does not mean to kill Tybalt. When he meets Tybalt and Mercutio quarreling in the street (III, i), he refuses to join in their fight. When he tries to make peace between them and Mercutio is fatally wounded, Romeo remarks pathetically, "I thought all for the best." Shortly thereafter Romeo does fight, and he kills Tybalt, but his immediate reaction—"O, I am fortune's fool"—shows that he does not feel responsible for the fatal error that will lead to the catastrophe.

If Romeo's character does have a tragic flaw, it is youthful impetuosity; an older or more deliberate man might somehow have managed to avoid the quarrel, and he would not rush to kill himself as soon as he believed Juliet was dead. And yet, that same youthful impetuosity is necessary if Romeo is to make the wholehearted commitment to romantic love that transforms him from the comic adolescent of the opening scene to the worthy object of love and lamentation at the end. The absolute romantic involvement this play celebrates would be impossible if the hero were older or less impetuous, more involved in worldly affairs or less impractical.

Keeping in mind conflicting arguments that the lovers are simply helpless victims of malevolent fate or that they (or at least Romeo) are responsible for their own doom, we may do best to reject both extremes or, rather, to attempt to subsume them both under another interpretation, namely, that the real agent of their deaths is neither a malevolent external fate nor an internal weakness in the protagonists but instead a love so overpowering that it is itself a kind of fate.

Death seems to be a necessary condition of absolute romantic love, not only here but in other love stories as diverse as Wagner's *Tristan und Isolde* and Erich Segal's *Love Story*. The interrelated imagery of love and death pervades *Romeo and Juliet,* and even the unimaginative Friar Laurence recognizes that procreation and death are inextricably connected in nature ("The earth, that's nature's mother, is her tomb./ What is her burying grave, that is her womb" [II, iii]). Moreover, we have only to imagine Romeo and Juliet long married and middle-aged discussing household affairs, to realize that their love in this play could not have persisted in the mortal world of time and change and physical necessity even if the lovers themselves had managed to survive. Any involement with worldly practicalities would have to dilute the intensity of their passion.

The lovers have to die so that they can become perfect embodiments of the love that moves them. Because Romeo and Juliet are young and unformed and impetuous, they give themselves wholeheartedly to their love and allow it to possess them entirely. Their love is an expression of their characters, but by the end of the play it has so consumed them that they become identical with it and no longer exist as anything but lovers. Romeo symbolically anticipates this process when he tells Juliet, during the great balcony scene when they first declare their love, "Call me but love, and I'll be new baptiz'd:/Henceforth I never will be Romeo" (II, ii).

Of all Shakespeare's tragedies, *Romeo and Juliet* depends most upon its poetry. The play is usually dated in the mid 1590s, when Shakespeare was probably writing his sonnets and those other preeminently lyrical plays, the history *Richard II* and the comedy *A Midsummer-Night's Dream*. In no other tragedy does Shakespeare use the imagery and the elaborate rhymed verse of lyric poetry to the extent he does in *Romeo and Juliet*. One useful approach to this play is, in fact, to regard it as a poem—a great, lyrical, metaphorical definition of romantic love. Imagery of

The balcony scene (II, ii) from *Romeo and Juliet,* played
by Laurence Olivier as Romeo and Vivien Leigh as Juliet
in a 1940 New York production of the play, directed by
Olivier at the 51st Street Theatre.

darkness and light, of night and day, pervades the language, and it serves more than anything else to define the nature of the lovers' passion.

Both lovers clearly prefer night to day. Juliet's passionate apostrophe to night in Act III, scene ii ("Gallop apace, you fiery-footed steeds,/Towards Phoebus' lodging") is only one of many passages in which they associate their longing for each other with a longing for night. Since their love has to be secret, there is an obvious literal reason why they must wait for nighttime to be together, but her passionate yearning for night goes far beyond the practical need for secrecy:

> Come, night; come, Romeo; come, thou day
>   in night;
> For thou wilt lie upon the wings of night
> Whiter than new snow on a raven's back.
> Come, gentle night, come, loving, black-
>   brow'd night,
> Give me my Romeo; and, when he shall die,
> Take him and cut him out in little stars,
> And he will make the face of heaven so fine
> That all the world will be in love with night
> And pay no worship to the garish sun.

Juliet associates night with death as well as love, and she pictures Romeo as a bright light shining in utter darkness, just as he pictures her when he first sees her at the Capulets' ball (I, v):

> O, she doth teach the torches to burn bright!
> It seems she hangs upon the cheek of night
> As a rich jewel in an Ethiop's ear;
> Beauty too rich for use, for earth too dear!

As both these passages show (Juliet's by explicit statement and Romeo's by the implications of "beauty

... for earth too dear"), one function of the night imagery is to reinforce the association between love and death that characterizes Romeo's and Juliet's passion from the very beginning.

When Juliet hears the news that Romeo has been banished, she says, "I'll to my wedding-bed;/And death, not Romeo, take my maidenhead!" (III, ii). When Friar Laurence hears it, he says, "Romeo/ ... / Affliction is enamour'd of thy parts,/And thou art wedded to calamity" (III, iii). When old Capulet thinks Juliet has died (IV, v), he tells Paris, "O son! the night before thy wedding-day/Hath Death lain with thy wife. . . ./Death is my son-in-law, death is my heir," and he gives detailed directions for transforming the marriage feast into a funeral, thus anticipating the real marriage in death that Romeo and Juliet will shortly enter.

Romeo's final speech has a poetic power that Capulet's words never attain, but he repeats Capulet's imagery although he does transform it:

> Shall I believe
> That unsubstantial Death is amorous
> And that the lean abhorred monster keeps
> Thee here in dark to be his paramour?
> For fear of that, I still will stay with thee,
> And never from this palace of dim night
> Depart again. . . .
>   . . . Eyes, look your last!
> Arms, take your last embrace! and lips, O you
> The doors of breath, seal with a righteous kiss
> A dateless bargain to engrossing death!
>
> (V, iii)

The many associations in the play between love and death emphasize not only the biological relationship that Friar Laurence describes but also a psychological one. Romantic love is traditionally seen as a loss of self, and the "new baptism" Romeo wishes for in the balcony scene can only occur when a kind of psychological death has destroyed the old self. When Romeo and Juliet kill themselves for love, their action is a great theatrical metaphor for the psychological dissolution and annihilation of self that are involved, even in the real world, in wholehearted submission to romantic love.

As well as being a metaphor for death, night also distinguishes the private, personal world of the lovers from the public world of reason, law, and social responsibility, which Shakespeare associates here, and in a number of other plays as well, with the light of day. The characters in *Romeo and Juliet* who support the values of the public world prefer day to night. To Friar Laurence, "the grey-ey'd morn smiles on the frowning night," while Romeo sees the light of dawn as "envious streaks" (III, v). Old Capulet calls for "more light" at his party (I, v), and Juliet's nurse's first important speech is a long reminiscence of a day when she sat "in the sun under the dove-house wall" (I, iii). The only thing Romeo and Juliet ever do together in the daylight is marry, and the marriage represents their, and Friar Laurence's, impossible attempt to establish their love as a social fact in the daylight world of law and responsibility. The necessary locale for their love, as their metaphors for it show from the first, is the infinite darkness of private, emotional experience, not the bright light of the finite social world. Coming from the wedding, Romeo becomes involved in the fatal duel with Tybalt: the lovers' attempt to establish their relationship in the daylight world has involved them in malignant fortune, and now they will have to die to escape its power.

The lovers do have an effect on the daylight world, but only after they leave it. The nurse foreshadows this impact when she discovers Juliet apparently dead on the morning of the day she is to marry Paris: "O woeful, woeful, woeful day!" she cries,

> Most lamentable day, most woeful day,
> That ever, ever I did yet behold!
> O day! O day! O day! O hateful day!
> Never was seen so black a day as this.
> O woeful day, O woeful day!
>
> (IV, v)

As the end of the play, when both lovers are indeed dead, the Prince says: "A glooming peace this morning with it brings;/The sun, for sorrow, will not show his head." At this point, the representatives of the daylight world have repudiated their daylight norms of division and quarreling to mourn the dead lovers and plan to immortalize them in statues of gold—the pure, imperishable metal that symbolizes immortal love.

And yet, although the lovers reject day for night and associate their love with darkness, they also associate it with light. Romeo calls Juliet's grave a lantern, for "her beauty makes this vault a feasting presence full of light" (V, iii). Juliet imagines Romeo dead and "cut/... out in little stars" that will light up the night (III, ii), and Romeo's first response to Juliet is that she teaches the very "torches to burn bright" (I, v). In fact, the characteristic image for their love is that of a bright light shining briefly in the darkness—a lantern, a flash of lightning, or an explosion of gunpowder. The darkness is needed to show the light: "lights by day," as Mercutio points out (I, iv), are wasted, for they cannot be seen. Similarly, the bright splendor of Romeo and Juliet's love is contingent upon its awful brevity. Friar Laurence warns Romeo against immoderate haste: "These violent delights have violent ends,/And in their triumph die, like fire and powder,/Which as they kiss consume" (II, vi). From a worldly point of view, he is perfectly right. The total effect of

Romeo and Juliet, however, engages the audience in the unworldly point of view that makes the lovers incapable of following his wise advice.

Some critics have argued that Friar Laurence's view is meant to be definitive. It seems best, however, to group Friar Laurence with Mercutio and Juliet's nurse as a slightly comic character, well intentioned toward the lovers, but finally unable to appreciate the transcendent quality of their love.

Of the three, Mercutio is most hostile to the love, and he knows least about it. In fact, when he laughs at Romeo's lovesickness, he thinks that Romeo is still infatuated with Rosaline, and his literal mistake about the facts, as is often the case in Shakespeare's plays, expresses an intrinsic limitation in his point of view. Just as Mercutio's literal ignorance confuses Juliet with Rosaline, his cynical view of sexual passion reduces love to infatuation.

Mercutio's bawdy jokes are still ringing in the audience's ears at the beginning of the balcony scene, but it may well be that they do not diminish but actually intensify the love scene that follows.[1] Mercutio's ironic disparagement of romantic love serves as a kind of lightning rod to deflect the cynicism members of the audience may bring with them to the theater. He says the worst that can be said about love, and the most sophisticated and skeptical of us can add nothing further. Moreover, Mercutio's stating the case against love gives Shakespeare a chance to refute it, which he does in several ways. First, he has Mercutio mistaken about the identity of Romeo's love. Second, the arrangement of characters—so that Mercutio, looking for Romeo, will be unable to find him, while Romeo, hidden, can see Mercutio—suggests (not logically but psychologically) that Romeo is generally more knowledgeable, perhaps about love as well as location. Finally, after Mercutio leaves the stage, Shakespeare has Romeo answer him: "He jests at scars that never felt a wound" (II, ii). Mercutio's jokes depend upon a detached, ironic contemplation of love, but Romeo's poetry in the scene that follows will involve the audience in his own passionate feeling.

Mercutio has an important role in the play, for he represents a comic reality principle that opposes the romantic extravagance of the main action and forces it to prove its validity. He mocks the irrational excesses of dreamers and lovers, and he is still able to jest at scars—even at death itself—after he has felt his own fatal wound. Moreover, Mercutio does not simply make fun of love and lovers; he also mocks love poetry itself, the main vehicle by which Shakespeare communicates Romeo's love to the audience. He ironically conjures Romeo to

> Speak but one rhyme, and I am satisfied;
> Cry but "Ay me!" pronounce but "love" and
>   "dove."
>
> (II, i)

He runs through the clichés of conventional love poetry:

> Alas, poor Romeo! he is already dead; stabb'd through with a white wench's black eye; run through the ear with a love song; the very pin of his heart cleft with the blind bow-boy's butt-shaft. . . .
>
> (II, iv)

And he uses his own sarcastic prose to mock the extravagant claims of conventional Renaissance love sonnets:

> Now is he for the numbers that Petrarch flowed in. Laura to his lady was a kitchen-

> wench (marry, she had a better love to be-
> rhyme her); Dido a dowdy; Cleopatra a gipsy;
> Helen and Hero hildings and harlots; Thisbe, a
> grey eye or so, but not to the purpose.
>
> (II, iv)

Still, Mercutio's parodies do not really discredit the kind of poetry in which Romeo expresses his love for Juliet. When Romeo describes his infatuation with Rosaline, he uses the formulas of the conventional Petrarchan sonnet:

> Love is a smoke made with the fume of sighs;
> Being purg'd, a fire sparkling in lovers' eyes;
> Being vex'd, a sea nourish'd with lovers' tears.
>
> (I, i)

These lines, and many more like them in the first act of *Romeo and Juliet*, sound as if they might come from a collection of minor, and deservedly forgotten, Elizabethan sonnets. One has only to contrast them with the passages in which Romeo declares his love for Juliet to see the difference between the object of Mercutio's mockery and the subject of Shakespeare's celebration. Mercutio's perspective is rationalistic and detached; his bawdy jokes assume that romantic passion is nothing more than the rationalization (or sublimation of a physical appetite. But living as he does in the daylight world of common reason, Mercutio can neither follow the lovers into the dark nor understand what they experience there.

Mercutio is Romeo's friend, but he is finally, although unwittingly, the cause of Romeo's banishment and death. The feud he helps reactivate threatens Romeo's and Juliet's love in the action of the play just as his jokes threaten to discredit it in the opinion of the audience. And yet, in both cases, Mercutio's threats serve finally to validate the love he can neither feel nor understand. The quality of Romeo's love poetry is proved by withstanding the test of Mercutio's satire, and the quality of Romeo's love is proved by his willingness to die for it. The fickle appetite with which Mercutio confuses it is selfish, but Romeo's death establishes the utter separateness of his love from the daylight domain of the transient, the appetitive, and the selfish.

Although the nurse and Mercutio do not like each other, they are similar in a number of ways. The nurse is Juliet's best friend, as Mercutio is Romeo's, and like him she is finally unable to appreciate her charge's love, even though she thinks she understands it perfectly. Just as Mercutio cannot tell the difference between Romeo's feeling for Rosaline and his feeling for Juliet, the nurse thinks Paris will satisfy Juliet as well as Romeo. She lacks Mercutio's quick wit and sophistication, but she too makes bawdy jokes about love: like him, she has a detached, and therefore a comic, view of it.

To be sure, the nurse's loquacity is clumsy rather than ingenious, and she judges by common sense rather than wit. But just as Mercutio, wishing Romeo well, hopes to cure him of his silly infatuation, the nurse, wishing Juliet well, hopes to settle her in a happy and respectable marriage. She can go further with the lovers than Mercutio can because she wants a bit more than satisfaction of sexual appetite for them, but when Romeo is banished and old Capulet determines to marry Juliet to Paris, the nurse replies to Juliet's anguished plea for comfort with:

> I think it best you married with the County.
> O, he's a lovely gentleman!
> Romeo's a dishclout to him. An eagle, madam,
> Hath not so green, so quick, so fair an eye
> As Paris hath. Beshrew my very heart,

> I think you are happy in this second match,
> For it excels your first; or if it did not,
> Your first is dead; or 'twere as good he were
> As living here and you no use of him.
>
> (III, v)

The nurse tries to persuade Juliet that a banished husband is as good as none at all, for he cannot give her the worldly status or the sexual pleasure that, in the nurse's view, make up the sum of a husband's "use." Her well-intentioned practical advice is as misguided as Mercutio's cynical jokes, for it shows her total inability to understand the nature of Juliet's love for Romeo. She thinks it is a matter of sexual appetite, which one man will satisfy as well as another. The word "use," which also appears as a metaphor for sexual relationships in Romeo's descriptions of Rosaline, sums up the worldly, exploitative conception of love that Romeo repudiates in his very first reaction to Juliet, when he calls her beauty "too rich for use, for earth too dear" (I, v).

Juliet rejects the nurse's advice (and the nurse as well: "Go, counsellor;/Thou and my bosom henceforth shall be twain") and turns to Friar Laurence for help in her desperate situation (III, v). But even the friar proves inadequate. He extols reason and moderation, higher values than Mercutio's amoral wit and the nurse's earthy common sense; but he still belongs, as they do, to the daylight world, and, like them, he finally deserts the lovers as they rush into the dark. What the friar wants for both lovers is holy matrimony (unlike the nurse, he does take their marriage vows seriously), and a settlement of their families' feud. But he still underestimates the quality of their love, which transcends death as well as sexual appetite and social prosperity; and it is significant that he finally fails them by running from the place of death, the

Capulets' tomb. He repeatedly counsels, "wisely and slow; they stumble that run fast," but it is he who runs at the crucial moment.

In a sense, Mercutio, the nurse, and Friar Laurence are right. Romantic love is not rational or practical or moderate. It is difficult to value a love that leaps into being at first sight and impels its victims to sacrifice their very lives within less than a week. But even if Romeo's and Juliet's passion seems subrational at the beginning, and even though we often assent to the daylight characters' well-taken criticism of the lovers' foolishness, by the end of the play their willingness to die for their love establishes it as a value transcending the rational norm that seemed to discredit it. The final lines belong to the prince, the highest representative in the play of law and order and rationality, and he pays tribute there to the worth of the lovers and the woefulness of their story.

By dying for love, Romeo and Juliet end their families' feud, and they gain an everlasting memorial—in the gold statues their parents will erect and in the play Shakespeare wrote. By braving the dark, they leave their mark upon the daylight world. In the same way, Shakespeare uses the opposition of the rational, daylight characters to prove the worth of Romeo's and Juliet's irrational passion. In fact, the entire play works by paradox and antithesis, from the paradoxical union of love and death that defines the lovers' passion to the opposed imagery of darkness and light in which they express it. In *Romeo and Juliet* Shakespeare transforms paradox—the hackneyed rhetorical strategy of a thousand Renaissance sonnets—into a principle of dramatic structure for a work that, although not among his greatest tragedies, is one of the greatest of all love poems.

Julius Caesar

In direct contrast to *Romeo and Juliet*, Shakespeare's next tragedy, *Julius Caesar*, centers on political and ideological issues rather than private, personal emotions. Its language is oratorical, not lyrical. The two famous orations over Caesar's corpse in Act III, scene ii, epitomize the style of the entire play: the rhyme, the elaborate metaphors, and the other kinds of verbal decoration in *Romeo and Juliet* are absent, and the characters often express themselves in long, formal speeches, even in informal situations.

Julius Caesar is the first of Shakespeare's so-called "Roman plays," based upon Sir Thomas North's translation of Plutarch's *Lives*, and in it Shakespeare seems to be making a conscious effort to evoke, and to comment upon, the civilization of ancient Rome. The play does not present a literal picture of classical Rome (even though some modern productions have at-

Portions of this chapter originally appeared in my article "The Pride of Shakespeare's Brutus," *Library Chronicle*, Winter, 1966, pp. 18–30. I am indebted to the editor, William E. Miller, for permission to use those sections here.

tempted to do so), for Shakespeare's practice here, as in his English history plays, was to attempt to capture the spirit of a time and place but not to reconstruct its material existence with literal-minded antiquarian exactness. Elizabethan historians did not approach the past with detailed, scientific objectivity. Instead, they looked to it for lessons about the present. In the same way, Shakespeare approaches the past in *Julius Caesar* not as an exercise in historical reconstruction but as an exploration of political and moral issues that held an immediate interest for Elizabethan Englishmen.

Both factions in the play are devoted to the state, but their concepts of the body politic, and of the best form of government for it, differ. The conspirators, especially Brutus, act in the name of a republican ideal based on the assumption that every citizen has equal freedom and dignity. Cassius says:

> I had as lief not be as live to be
> In awe of such a thing as I myself.
> I was born free as Caesar, so were you;
> We both have fed as well, and we can both
> Endure the winter's cold as well as he.
>
> (I, ii)

The monarchial ideal, in contrast, assumes the fallibility of ordinary human beings and demands that they submit for their own good and that of the state to a higher and better power than individuals can muster to govern themselves. It is based upon the commonplace analogy between the individual and the body politic—the notion that the king must control the state in the same way the individual's nobler reason must control the baser passions, that the organization of a good state, no less than the constitution of a good person, is necessarily hierarchical.

Ironically, Brutus uses the analogy between the

"state of a man" and that of a kingdom to describe his own troubled response to Cassius's suggestion that he join the conspiracy:

> Since Cassius first did whet me against Caesar,
> I have not slept.
> Between the acting of a dreadful thing
> And the first motion, all the interim is
> Like to a phantasma or a hideous dream.
> The Genius and the mortal instruments
> Are then in council; and the state of a man,
> Like to a little kingdom, suffers then
> The nature of an insurrection.
>
> (II, i)

Brutus is the best intentioned of all the conspirators, but he is so thoroughly devoted to the republican ideal that he fails to recognize the implications his analogy has for the state. In the state, he assumes, the insurrection will bring peace and good order.

Antony, the chief exponent of the monarchial ideal, uses the traditional analogy to prophesy after Caesar's assassination:

> A curse shall light upon the limbs of men:
> Domestic fury and fierce civil strife
> Shall cumber all the parts of Italy;
> Blood and destruction shall be so in use
> And dreadful objects so familiar
> That mothers shall but smile when they behold
> Their infants quartered with the hands of war.
>
> (III, i)

The bloody destruction visited upon the head of state will spread to its lower parts; just as Caesar has been butchered, so will the state he represents and its human members.

Brutus' method of argument, like his views, directly

contrasts with Antony's. Brutus enjoins his fellow conspirators to "be sacrificers, but not butchers," reminding them that they oppose only the "spirit of Caesar" and not the man himself (II, i). That "Caesar must bleed for it" is only an unfortunate necessity, required by their high purpose but not really involved in it, for "in the spirit of men there is no blood" (II, i). Later, standing with bloody hands beside Caesar's bleeding corpse, Brutus tells Antony to disregard the evidence of his senses:

> yet see you but our hands
> And this the bleeding business they have done.
> Our hearts you see not; they are pitiful;
> And pity to the general wrong of Rome
> . . . .
> Hath done this deed on Caesar.
>
> (III, i)

To Antony, however, Caesar's corpse remains a "bleeding piece of earth," and the conspirators *are* "butchers." Disregarding Brutus' rational arguments about the good of the state, he responds instead to the physical spectacle before him. More impressed by empirical evidence than logical reasons, Antony sees the situation, and the state, in analogical, monarchial terms.

Brutus, on the other hand, repeatedly discounts personal and particular considerations in favor of general principles. In deciding to join the conspiracy (II, i), he considers that he knows "no personal cause to spurn at" Caesar but only "the general." After the assassination he tells Antony, "Our reasons are so full of good regard/That were you, Antony, the son of Caesar,/You should be satisfied" (III, i); and even though Antony does not respond as Brutus expects to "reasons," he does acknowledge, even at the end, that Brutus was guided by them and joined the conspiracy "in a general honest thought" and not out of personal

envy or ambition (V, v). Brutus is so certain that abstract principle is sufficient to guide human conduct
that he rejects Cassius's suggestion that the conspirators
swear their resolution to each other. To him a personal
covenant means far less than the abstract arguments
and the general concept of Roman honor that lead him
to kill his beloved Caesar for what he regards as the
good of the state.

The differences between Brutus and Antony are
most apparent in the two orations in Act III. Brutus
speaks in prose, and Antony in verse. Brutus argues
abstractly, and Antony points to physical evidence.
Brutus appeals to his hearers' reason, and Antony, who
shows and describes rather than simply arguing, appeals to their emotions. Brutus discounts his friendship
for Caesar and emphasizes the good of the state ("Not
that I lov'd Caesar less, but that I lov'd Rome more").
Antony emphasizes Caesar's friendship ("He was my
friend, faithful and just to me"), his own love and
grief, and Caesar's love for the common people. The
mob is won by Antony's appeal, but even before
Antony speaks, it is apparent that Brutus has failed to
reach them. Brutus ends his oration with the promise,
"as I slew my best lover for the good of Rome, I have
the same dagger for myself, when it shall please my
country to need my death." The mob, oblivious to all
his arguments, replies by shouting, "Let him be Caesar," ironically revealing their continued need for and
allegiance to the Caesar principle from which Brutus
hoped to free them when he slew his "best lover."

Although the play is called *The Tragedy of Julius
Caesar*, most critics agree that Brutus is actually the
tragic hero. It is difficult to understand Brutus' tragedy,
however, without considering Caesar's first, for the
two are closely related, symbolically as well as dramatically.

Caesar is the "foremost man of all this world" (IV,

iii), but he suffers from a monstrous pride that Shakespeare emphasizes by coupling Caesar's expressions of it with evidence of his physical weakness. Shortly after Cassius describes the way he had to save Caesar from drowning in the Tiber (I, ii), Caesar enters with an obsequious train, delivers himself of the famous sententious observations about the characteristics of lean men and fat ones, and concludes,

> I rather tell thee what is to be fear'd
> Than what I fear; for always I am Caesar.
>
> (I, ii)

But this is not the end of the speech. Caesar's next line, "Come on my right hand, for this ear is deaf," provides an ironic anticlimax to his pretentious claims.

As the action develops, Caesar proceeds from pretentiousness to outright hubris. When the augurers' portents warn him against going to the senate, he decides to go anyway, saying:

> Danger knows full well
> That Caesar is more dangerous than he.
> We are two lions litter'd in one day,
> And I the elder and more terrible.
>
> (II, ii)

And just before the assassination, he rejects the petition to enfranchise Publius Cimber with the splendidly worded but monstrous claim:

> I could well be mov'd, if I were as you;
> If I could pray to move, prayers would move
>   me;
> But I am constant as the northern star,
> Of whose true-fix'd and resting quality
> There is no fellow in the firmament.
> ....
> So in the world; 'tis furnish'd well with men,

And men are flesh and blood, and apprehen-
sive;
Yet in the number I do know but one
That unassailable holds on his rank,
Unshak'd of motion; and that I am he.

(III, i)

In this speech, Caesar denies that he shares the common
weakness of mortal men. It is dramatically appropriate
that he is killed immediately thereafter.

This pride of Caesar's serves to draw the audience
into complicity with the conspirators, for it makes
the audience desire the assassination and enables them
to accept it emotionally. It also prepares the audience
to understand what happens to Brutus during the
course of the play and to accept the necessity that he
too must fall. For Brutus is also guilty of pride, even
though his pride is much less obvious than Caesar's,
and even though Shakespeare defines it in terms of
ethical and political ideas that are no longer familiar.

Many modern critics have seen Brutus as a misguided
idealist, incompetent in practical politics but ruled by
the best of motives. They often note that he displays
some of the unpleasant self-righteousness that often
accompanies extreme devotion to abstract ideals. But
set within the context of Elizabethan ideology, Brutus'
self-righteousness and his political miscalculations indicate a clearly defined moral failing.

Before the assassination, Brutus uses the traditional
analogy between the head of state and the head of the
body to reject Cassius' suggestion that they kill Antony
as well as Caesar. Antony will be powerless after Caesar is killed, Brutus predicts, because he "is but a limb
of Caesar" and therefore "can do no more than Caesar's arm/When Caesar's head is off" (II, i). But there
is another way of reading the analogy: Antony predicts over Caesar's corpse that "a curse shall light upon

the limbs of men" (III, i), and his own transformation from the good fellow of Act I into the treacherous demagogue of the funeral oration and the cold-blooded political manipulator of Act IV seems to fulfill his prophecy.

Brutus' failure to foresee Antony's behavior can be seen as a failure to understand the implications of his own metaphor. Although Brutus describes Antony as Caesar's limb, he feels that he can do the limb a service by cutting off the head: he tells the plebeians that Antony, like them, "shall receive the benefit" of Caesar's death, "a place in the commonwealth" (III, ii). But his own metaphor should have told him (and certainly told Shakespeare's audience) that neither Antony nor the plebeians could benefit from the assassination. Antony's grief for Caesar and the change in Antony's character both show, in different ways, how much he suffers from Caesar's murder. Similarly, the plebeians are transformed by it from the comic revelers in the opening scene to the wild mob in the third act that tears a poet to pieces simply because he bears the same name as one of the conspirators. At the beginning of the play the plebeians are identified by occupation, and the identifications are themselves evidence of order in the state. By the end of Antony's oration, they have become an undifferentiated rabble, ready to "pluck down forms, windows, anything" (III, ii). Antony's comment, "Mischief, thou art afoot," suggests the evil of which the lowest elements (the feet) of the body politic are capable once they have lost their head.

Politically, Brutus' greatest error is allowing Antony to deliver his funeral oration. But Brutus' political miscalculation here, like his decision to let Antony live, his decision to join the conspiracy, and his political philosophy itself, is finally a more-than-political matter; it is the product of a misconception of human nature as it is depicted in the play, the evidence of a blindness to the moral structure of the universe in which Shakespeare places him.

Brutus' misjudgment of the mob, his failure to provide in his political calculations for their irrationality, their propensity for evil, and their consequent need for control from above, stems from his misjudgment of human nature: he denies the power of the passions and the consequent inadequacy of natural philosophy unaided to deal with the human condition. He thinks Antony will accept the assassination once he hears the good reasons for it. To the mob, he says, "hear me for my cause." Many critics have remarked that Brutus' oration fails to reach the mob because it is designed for an audience of Brutuses. In fact, Brutus acts and judges as if he lived in a world of Brutuses, and he persists in this opinion even in the face of direct evidence to the contrary. When the mob shouts, "Let him be Caesar," Brutus shows himself as ignorant of their meaning as they are of his, for he leaves them alone in the forum to hear Antony (III, ii). At the end of his life, he declares, "My heart doth joy that yet in all my life/I found no man but he was true to me" (V, v). Antony's betrayal is fresh in the mind of the audience, if not of Brutus.

Brutus' pride, unlike the personal hubris of Caesar, is an inordinate faith in human goodness; it is the pride of the natural philosopher who feels that human reason is adequate to all things. In theological terms Brutus' error is his failure to recognize the existence of original sin and the consequent necessity for grace from above to do what human beings cannot do for themselves. In political terms it is his failure to recognize the weakness and inherent evil in the lower orders and the consequent necessity that they, too, must be governed by a higher power.

The hazards of applying Christian political and theological concepts to a play set in pre-Christian times are

obvious. The many orations in *Julius Caesar*, the grave
austerity of the style, and the frequent occurrence of
the words "Rome" and "Roman" all suggest a conscious effort to evoke a sense of the classical world.
The world evoked, however, is not the Rome of
modern classical historians. It is a world in which
clocks strike and men wear hats and Roman citizens
speak, if not like Elizabethans, still as an Elizabethan
imagined a Roman to speak. Shakespeare has not made
his Romans Elizabethans, but he has made his play a
comment on the Roman spirit from an Elizabethan
point of view.

Of all the characters, Brutus comes closest to achiev-
ing the Roman ideal of conduct as it was understood in
Elizabethan tradition and presented in this play. The
fact of Brutus' austere virtue is attested throughout: all the other characters acknowledge it, and
Antony's final statement (which, like his soliloquy
over Caesar's corpse and his oration in Act III, is
probably directed as much to the audience in the
theater as to the other characters on stage) sums up
Brutus' excellence; he is the epitome of natural virtue:

> This was the noblest Roman of them all.
> All the conspirators, save only he,
> Did that they did in envy of great Caesar;
> He only, in a general honest thought
> And common good to all, made one of them.
> His life was gentle, and the elements
> So mix'd in him that Nature might stand up
> And say to all the world, "This was a man!"
>
> (V, v)

And yet the very terms of Antony's praise served to
remind Shakespeare's audience that Brutus' virtue was
of a particular and limited sort. If he was the noblest
Roman of them all, he was still not nobler than the
Roman standard itself; and if "Nature might stand up/

And say to all the world, 'This was a man!' " Nature itself had certain limitations. To the Elizabethan Christians, Nature unredeemed by grace was "without force and effect,"[2] and the very perfection of Brutus' allegiance to the ideal of natural philosophy serves to demonstrate the inadequacy of that ideal as a guide for human conduct or a basis for political theory.

Brutus fails because he has too much faith in human righteousness: he refuses to recognize the human proclivity for sin and error. His fatal blindness is thus ironically similar to Caesar's fatal flaw—the refusal to recognize his own human limitations. Caesar's deafness and his susceptibility to the "falling sickness" remind the audience of the human fallibility that Caesar shares even as he denies he shares it. More subtly, Brutus' failure to recognize the political limitations of the populace and the limitations of human nature itself also reveal pride and moral blindness.

Brutus repeatedly insists upon disregarding the evidence of the senses; but human knowledge, no less than human nature, has certain limitations, and, failing to recognize them, Brutus is blinded by intellectual pride. He tells Antony to disregard the spectacle of the bloody conspirators (a spectacle visible to the audience as well as to Antony). Brutus assumes he can see and speak with absolute certainty about invisible things, that he can know essence directly (as only angels were believed to do), without depending upon the imperfect mediation of human vision or discursive reason. In rejecting the evidence of the senses, Brutus is attempting to transcend the limitations of his imperfect physical being.

Pride, then, is the defect in the idealistic vision that leads Brutus to join the conspiracy, for in making his decision, Brutus fails to recognize either the inadequacy of the lower elements in the body politic or the possibility that his own vision of what Caesar may become is mistaken. And once he joins the conspiracy, Brutus is placed in situations of ever-increasing pre-eminence and thus increasingly confirmed in his in-ordinate confidence in his own virtue and judgment. After the assassination, when the removal of Caesar's power transforms the plebeians into a dangerous mob, the triumvirs into cynical and ruthless manipulators, and Brutus' co-conspirators into corrupt takers of bribes, Brutus becomes so unequivocally the noblest Roman on the scene that he is increasingly confirmed in his pride.

Brutus is, to the end of the play, a supremely good man and a supreme exemplar of Roman virtue, but his very supremacy serves to reveal the deficiences of the virtue he exemplifies. It is in the name of Rome and the Roman values of freedom, honor, self-control, and self-determination that Cassius urges Brutus to join the conspiracy. Brutus finally decides to join in the name of Rome ("O Rome, I make thee promise," he says) in a speech where the word "Rome" occurs six times in the space of ten lines (II, i, 47–56). Ligarius swears "by all the gods that Romans bow before" to join the conspiracy and calls Brutus the "soul of Rome" (II, ii). Although the words "Rome" and "Roman" occur seventy-two times during the play, in the second half, from the end of Act III to Antony's final tribute to Brutus, they "occur only in the mouths of the rebels."[3] All these verbal associations tend to suggest that the conspiracy is a manifestation of "Romanness" and to imply that Brutus, when he becomes its guiding spirit, becomes also the leading manifestation of the soul of Rome.

At the beginning of the play, in a passage that is notable for punning in a play generally lacking in puns, Cassius describes Caesar's pride by saying, "Now is it Rome indeed and room enough, when there is in it but one only man" (I, ii; in Shakespeare's time, "Rome" was pronounced the same as "room"). He urges Brutus to join the conspiracy to destroy Caesar because Caesar, in his insufferable pride, will not leave room for anyone else to be a Roman. Brutus seems to accept his argument, for after the assassination he asks the plebeians, "Who is here so rude that would not be a Roman?" and he tells them that they will all receive, as the "benefit of his dying, a place in the commonwealth" (III, ii). Cassius also tells Brutus that "there was a Brutus once that would have brook'd th' eternal devil to keep his state in Rome/As easily as a king" (I, ii). Brutus joins the conspiracy, in effect, to banish the devil from Rome, for he sees Caesar's ambition as the only source of evil in an otherwise innocent situation. But the assassination does not banish the devil; instead it unleashes him, and even the noblest Roman of them all succumbs to the very failing that marred the greatness of the man he killed. The pride that was the fatal flaw in Caesar's greatness and in Rome's remains. The assassination of Caesar does not destroy this pride but serves instead to demonstrate the pervasiveness of its force and the multiplicity of its operations.

At the beginning of the play the proud Caesar is the "foremost man of all this world." By killing Caesar, Brutus acquires for a time the foremost position in the world of Rome and with it the pride that seems its inevitable accompaniment. There is an ironic ambiguity in Brutus' words to his fellow conspirators, "O, that we then could come by Caesar's spirit/And not dismember Caesar!" (II, i). After they do dismember Caesar, Brutus seems to "come by" Caesar's spirit in a way he never anticipated and never does recognize. This transference is shown symbolically in three significant incidents, in all of which Shakespeare altered the material he found in Plutarch. In the first of these incidents, immediately after the assassination, Brutus has the conspirators bathe their hands in Caesar's blood, an act which suggests a ritual assumption of Caesar's qualities. In the second, the mob responds to Brutus' oration by shouting, "Let him be Caesar," and, "Caesar's better parts shall be crown'd in Brutus." And in the third, the ghost who visits Brutus at Sardis, identifying himself as "thy evil spirit, Brutus," is also identified by Shakespeare as the ghost of Julius Caesar (IV, iii). The evil spirit that Brutus tried to kill when he stabbed his beloved Julius lives on, ironically in Brutus himself.

There are, however, important differences between Caesar's pride and Brutus'. Caesar's proud spirit makes him deny that he shares the common weakness of humankind, and it makes him absurdly oblivious to the implications of his own physical infirmities. Brutus, on the other hand, fails to recognize the common weakness itself, and his pride makes him tragically oblivious to the moral and intellectual infirmities of the lower parts of the body politic.

It is important to remember that the body politic is Rome and not England and that Brutus' pride, unlike Caesar's hubris, is not considered a failing by the other inhabitants of the pre-Christian world in which he is placed. But that very fact, although it helps to exonerate Brutus from some of the blame that would attach to him in an Elizabethan context, serves, in an Elizabethan theater, as an implicit comment on the limitations of his world.

Hamlet, Prince of Denmark

Hamlet's tragedy seems to defy critical explication. The very number of interpretations suggests that none of them is finally satisfactory, and the actors who have portrayed Hamlet over the years have been as divergent as the critics in their views of Hamlet's character and predicament. Perhaps we should all remember, as we approach this play, the warning Hamlet gives to Rosencrantz and Guildenstern in the famous "recorder speech" at the end of Act III, scene ii:

> Why, look you now, how unworthy a thing you make of me! You would play upon me, you would seem to know my stops, you would pluck out the heart of my mystery, you would sound me from my lowest note to the top of my compass. . . .

In their fascination with Hamlet's character and psychology, nineteenth-century critics tended to neglect his dramatic context, his interactions with the other characters, his overt acts, and the consequences those acts have in his world. For them, the Danish court was only a dim backdrop for Hamlet's internal struggles; the real drama was revealed in Hamlet's great soliloquies, and the rest of the dialogue and action served only to establish transitions and to provide occasions for those eloquent ventures in self-exploration.

Many modern critics have responded to the continued enigma of Hamlet's character and motivation by turning their attention from the prince to his dramatic context and focusing on the more accessible matters of dramatic tradition, structure, and imagery. The play does, in fact, have a recognizable structure, including a clearly defined Aristotelian "reversal" coupled with an equally clearly defined and equally Aristotelian "recognition."[4] Hamlet seems almost to have read Aristotle's *Poetics* when he says, after discovering that the unseen eavesdropper he killed was Polonius:

> For this same lord,
> I do repent; but Heaven hath pleas'd it so,
> To punish me with this and this with me,
> That I must be their scourge and minister.
> I will . . . answer well
> The death I gave him.
> . . . .
> Thus bad begins and worse remains behind.
>
> (III, iv)

This fatal error, he knows, will set off an inexorable process of tragic retribution.

The question of Hamlet's "tragic flaw"— the fault that is finally responsible for his downfall—has inspired endless debate, and Hamlet has been charged with procrastination, excessive conscientiousness, an intellectual's incapacity for action, melancholy, subconscious lust for his mother, insanity, and any number of other defects of character and personality. Aristotle's emphasis upon plot offers a good corrective to our own tendency to emphasize Hamlet's internal problems at the expense of the overt problems that define the movement of the plot. Aristotle's word for the tragic flaw, *hamartia*, was later used in the Greek Gospels to mean "sin," but in Aristotle's *Poetics* it seems to mean simply a mistake or a false step; and this meaning exactly fits Hamlet's murder of Polonius. Hamlet thought when he stabbed through the arras that he was killing Claudius, but the unfortunate eavesdropper was really Polonius, the father of Ophelia, and of Laertes, who will finally kill Hamlet.

Such an account of the reason for Hamlet's fall is obviously incomplete and superficial, but it does make a useful starting point for an analysis of the play's structure and for an elucidation of Hamlet's place within the moral world this structure helps to define. At the beginning the audience is introduced to Hamlet's world with a scene outside the Danish castle. Darkness, suspicion, and fear determine the behavior of the watch—and the initial impression the audience receives of Hamlet's world. A ghost appears, and the audience is convinced, before Hamlet ever appears on the scene that, as Marcellus will later say (I, iv), "Something is rotten in the state of Denmark." The opening lines of the play—"Who's there?" and "Nay, answer me. Stand, and unfold yourself"—establish the mood of suspicion and also serve to describe the action in the first half of the play. All the characters will be in the dark, suspecting each other and devising complicated stratagems to discover each other's hidden motives and secret deeds; but they will be equally careful to conceal their own, so that their attempts at discovery will serve only to intensify the confusion. The opening exchange in the dark between Bernardo and Francisco is a brief foretaste of the complicated, secret maneuvers that Hamlet and Claudius and Polonius and Rosencrantz and Guildenstern will execute throughout the first half of the play.

The second scene offers a sharp contrast to the first. The setting is inside the castle, the court is assembled, all but one of the actors wear bright costumes, and order and good cheer seem to prevail. Claudius opens the scene with a springtime metaphor—"Though yet of Hamlet our dear brother's death/The memory be green"—even though the real weather, as we learned in the previous scene, is wintry. Claudius speaks in measured blank verse, judiciously balancing "discretion" with "nature," wisdom with sorrow, "funeral" with "marriage," and "delight" with "dole" in, he says, "equal scale." When Laertes approaches, Claudius proclaims, "You cannot speak of reason to the Dane/And lose your voice," and he grants Laertes's request to return to France with the sunny words "Take thy fair hour, Laertes."

The atmosphere here is altogether pleasant and respectable. But the audience, unlike the courtiers on stage, is likely to be a bit suspicious of Claudius's sunny words, because the audience has seen the opening scene and experienced some of the dark world that Claudius attempts to deny.

Hamlet, who has not been present in scene i, seems to share the knowledge that this scene communicated to the audience. He seems terribly out of place among the contented courtiers, but the audience is more likely to identify with Hamlet's point of view than with theirs. Claudius's long first speech uses smooth rhetoric to reconcile irreconcilable opposites, and abstract terms to make his outrageous situation seem reasonable. But when Claudius addresses Hamlet, equally agreeably, with "my cousin Hamlet, and my son," and asks him, "How is it that the clouds still hang on you?," Hamlet responds with a bitter pun on Claudius's "clouds" and

In the first uncut staging of *Hamlet* in New York (in 1938, at the St. James Theatre) Maurice Evans played Hamlet under Margaret Webster's direction.

"son"—"Not so, my lord; I am too much i' th' sun"—simultaneously rejecting Claudius's sunny world and his offer of paternity. When Gertrude argues reasonably against excessive mourning, Hamlet passionately defends his "inky cloak" and "suits of solemn black" as the outward signs of an inner grief that "passeth show." Hamlet's black clothing, no less than his bitter grief, associates him with the cold night of the opening scene in opposition to the spurious brightness and warmth of Claudius's court.

At the end of the second scene Hamlet learns that an apparition resembling his father has appeared three times at midnight, and his excited reaction—"Foul deeds will rise,/Though all the earth o'erwhelm them, to men's eyes"—defines the expectations the first two scenes have generated in the audience, as well as Hamlet's own hopes.

The third scene, which introduces Polonius's family, may seem extraneous to the main plot, but it contributes to the growing atmosphere of suspicion and malaise. Laertes and Polonius warn Ophelia to be suspicious of Hamlet's courtship and to guard her chastity and reputation. Laertes warns her:

> Virtue itself scapes not calumnious strokes.
> The canker galls the infants of the spring
> Too oft before the buttons be disclos'd,
> And in the morn and liquid dew of youth
> Contagious blastments are most imminent.
> Be wary then; best safety lies in fear.

Ophelia responds with her own warning for Laertes:

> Do not, as some ungracious pastors do,
> Show me the steep and thorny way to heaven,
> Whilst, like a puff'd and reckless libertine,
> Himself the primrose path of dalliance treads,
> And recks not his own rede.

Then Polonius warns Laertes to be careful with his money and friendship and behavior and clothing when he returns to France. All these lectures and warnings manifest a distrust, not simply or even primarily of each other, but of human nature in general; and they serve to identify Polonius's rather ordinary bourgeois family with the corrupted atmosphere of the court at which he serves as Lord Chamberlain to the pleasant, plausible king.

In the fourth scene the ghost returns to tell his story to Hamlet; now the foul deeds do rise, and the canker that infects Claudius's court is identified as regicide. The pervasive mood of Act I has been one of mistrust —in the watchmen, in Hamlet, in Polonius's family, and in the audience. This final scene serves to confirm the suspicions and identify the source of the evil. If, as Hamlet says at the end of the scene, "the time is out of joint," the audience now knows why.

In Act II the atmosphere of suspicion persists, and in addition there is spying—the overt action that suspicion motivates. In the opening scene, Polonius, suspicious that Laertes may not be following his good advice, sends Reynaldo to Paris to spy on him. Lie about Laertes, he says, and slander him a little:

> Your bait of falsehood takes this carp of truth;
> And thus do we of wisdom and of reach,
> With windlasses and with assays of bias,
> By indirections find directions out.

Fishing for truth with falsehood is what all the characters will do in Act II, but their strategies will intensify, rather than dissipate, the uneasy atmosphere that troubles them all.

In the second scene of Act II Claudius and Gertrude set Rosencrantz and Guildenstern to spy on Hamlet and report back with their discoveries. Polonius plots with Claudius and Gertrude to spy on Hamlet, using Ophelia as bait: "I'll loose my daughter to him," he proposes; "Be you and I behind an arras then" to "mark the encounter." Hamlet pretends to be mad to confound his enemies and then orders a play to try to discover the truth about his father's murder, for he is suspicious of the ghost as well as Claudius ("The

spirit that I have seen may be the devil . . . and perhaps
. . . abuses me to damn me"). Like all the others, Hamlet is using false appearances and "indirections" in his
effort to discover the truth about the trouble in Denmark.

While Act I is characterized by suspicion and Act II
by spying, Act III is devoted to seeing. The first scene
opens with Rosencrantz and Guildenstern reporting to
the King and Queen. Then Polonius and Claudius prepare to eavesdrop upon Hamlet's interview with
Ophelia. Setting the stage, Polonius tells Ophelia to
read a devotional book, and, characteristically, he offers
a platitudinous comment: "We are oft to blame in
this,—/'Tis too much prov'd—that with devotion's
visage/And pious action we do sugar o'er/The devil
himself." The king's response, heard only by the
audience—"How smart a lash that speech doth give
my conscience!/The harlot's cheek, beautied with
plast'ring art,/Is not more ugly to the thing that helps
it/Than is my deed to my most painted word"—is
the first clear evidence of his guilt. The ghost, as Hamlet said, might have been a deceitful, diabolical spirit,
and some modern critics and directors have even dis-
missed him as a hallucination projected by Hamlet's
disturbed psyche. But Claudius's admission of his guilt
supports the ghost's veracity and begins the series of
revelations in Act III that will satisfy the doubts and
suspicions which the audience, along with Hamlet, has
been suffering so far.

Next, Polonius and the king do their spying, and although Hamlet seems to be aware of their presence,
he says enough to let the king see that Hamlet is
neither lovesick nor insane, but troubled with thoughts
that offer some danger to Claudius's own safety.

In the second scene, the process of seeing reaches its
height. Here, Hamlet stages his "mousetrap," the play
that dramatizes Claudius's crime and at the same time

threatens Hamlet's vengeance: the murder is performed just as Claudius committed it, but the killer is
not the victim's brother, but his nephew. The play lets
Claudius see clearly that Hamlet knows his guilt, and
Claudius's response lets Hamlet see that he is indeed
guilty. In addition, the player king's comments on the
universality of change, loss, and betrayal extend the
implications of the action beyond Claudius and Hamlet
to everyone who watches and hears, the audience in
the theater no less than the Danish courtiers on stage.

Hamlet planned his play to "catch the conscience of
the king" because he had "heard that guilty creatures
sitting at a play/Have by the very cunning of the
scene/Been struck so to the soul that presently/They
have proclaim'd their malefactions" (II, ii).[5] There was
likely to be some ambiguity in Shakespeare's theater
about the identity of the guilty creatures sitting at the
play, for if Claudius was watching the players, he was
himself a "player king," and Hamlet and the Danish
court watched him as well as the players. But on
Shakespeare's stage, Hamlet was acted by a player,
and the audience stationed around the stage was simply
the outermost edge of a series of watchers of plays.
The process of seeing undisclosed guilt here reaches
beyond the confines of the stage to implicate the audience directly and painfully in the tragic action.

The play within the play is the climax of the series
of revelations in the third act, for it is the most
graphic, and it has the widest implications; but the
remainder of the act brings additional revelations of
hidden guilt. Hamlet reveals to Rosencrantz and Guildenstern that he knows they are liars, the king's prayer
scene confirms to the audience that he is guilty of
murder as well as incest, and when Hamlet answers
Gertrude's summons to her closet, he attempts to "set
[her] up a glass where [she] may see" her "inmost

part." He reveals Claudius's crime to her, he forces her to look at pictures of his father and of Claudius, and he delivers an impassioned sermon to make her see the viciousness of her new marriage. Gertrude replies:

> O Hamlet, speak no more!
> Thou turn'st mine eyes into my very soul,
> And there I see such black and grained spots
> As will not leave their tinct.
>
> (III, iv)

Hamlet has succeeded in making his mother see her wretched condition, but before he leaves her chamber, he must suffer an unwelcome revelation of his own.

Hamlet has delayed killing Claudius until he could be sure of the facts. Maybe the ghost was a demonic spirit preying upon his melancholy with false accusations against a king who smiled, spoke fair and reasonable words, and enjoyed the love of Hamlet's mother and the loyalty of the court. Hamlet wanted to act in perfect conscience and to control the consequences of his acts as well. To kill the king at prayer might, if the king were truly repenting, send his soul to heaven, so Hamlet waited for a better moment.

That moment seems to come when Hamlet hears a voice behind the arras in Gertrude's closet, and he stabs through it to kill the king; but when he looks to see what he has done, he discovers Polonius. And so Hamlet, too, is caught in the web of crime, guilt, and retribution that has ensnared the Danish court. The irony is horrifying: for three acts, Hamlet has taken extraordinary pains to test the situation and examine his conscience in order to avoid acting without sufficient knowledge—to avoid, that is, making a stab in the dark. And when he finally does act against the king, he does stab in the dark, and, tragically, he kills the wrong man.

Hamlet's first reaction to the sight of Polonius's body is one of ruthless incomprehension:

> Thou wretched, rash, intruding fool, farewell!
> I took thee for thy better. Take thy fortune.
> Thou find'st to be too busy is some danger.
>
> (III, iv)

But before the end of the scene, he sees more clearly what he has done. He still dismisses Polonius as a "foolish, prating knave," but now he knows he will suffer the consequences of his crime, and he repents the killing. The action, in Aristotle's terms, has now "veered round to its opposite": Hamlet will now be the guilty object of Laertes's vengeance for a murdered father and not simply the innocent seeker of revenge for his own father's death.

After Hamlet kills Polonius, but before he recognizes the full consequences of his act, the ghost returns "to whet" Hamlet's "almost blunted purpose." Gertrude is spared the sight of the ghost. I see "nothing at all," she says, "yet all that is I see" (III, iv). Some critics have argued that Gertrude's response proves that this apparition is a figment of Hamlet's imagination, but Gertrude's failure to see the ghost may simply betoken her lack of moral sensitivity; she has, after all, also failed to see her own crimes, and her new husband's nature, and the true situation in Denmark, until Hamlet forces her to recognize them.

Hamlet's recognition of his own guilt, together with this final appearance of the ghost, marks the turning point in the action. From here on, the characters will be engaged in plots to destroy their enemies, for the revelations in Act III have eliminated the need for further spying. Now Claudius plots to have Hamlet killed in England, and Hamlet resolves, "from this time forth,/My thoughts be bloody, or be nothing worth!"

(IV, iv). The last two acts of the play are taken up with suffering and retribution.

Laertes, Gertrude, Hamlet, and Claudius all die by poison, as did Hamlet's father. In fact, the symbolic center of the play, as it is the impetus for the action, is King's Hamlet's description of his murder (I, v). What Claudius has done to the king, he has also done to the kingdom. "It's given out," the ghost tells Hamlet, "that, sleeping in mine orchard,/A serpent stung me; so the whole ear of Denmark/Is by a forged process of my death/Rankly abus'd." The Elizabethan analogy between the human body and the body politic, which helped to define the mystical relationship between a king and his kingdom, serves here to indicate that the poisoning of the king's body was the cause and model of the corruption of his kingdom. The king, as Laertes says (I, iii), is the "head" of the state, the state is his "body," and its "sanity and health" depend on him.

The ghost's allusions to the orchard and the serpent ("the serpent that did sting thy father's life/Now wears his crown") suggest an additional analogy, associating Claudius's crime with the archetypal act of corruption performed by the serpent in the garden of Eden. The play is full of images of poison, disease, and decay, and of allusions to the infinite corruptibility of human nature. These images and allusions serve to corroborate Hamlet's belief that Denmark is a paradigm of the whole fallen world. "Denmark's a prison," Hamlet says to Rosencrantz and Guildenstern. "Then is the world one," says Rosencrantz. "A goodly one," Hamlet replies, "in which there are many confines, wards, and dungeons, Denmark being one of the worst" (II, ii).

Like the agency of poison, the agency of Claudius's evil is hidden and secret. Claudius is a "smiling villain," whose lies and flattery, like his poison, go in through the ears. Also like poison, they work by corrupting from within rather than by attacking and destroying from without. Claudius has won over the Danish court, beginning with the queen, to the point that when the play opens only Hamlet resists his blandishments, and even Hamlet thinks he may be mistaken about the seemingly good king. Polonius, Laertes, Ophelia, and Rosencrantz and Guildenstern all cooperate with Claudius, not under coercion but under the influence of his plausible words and his usurped authority as king.

The poison Claudius poured into the king's ear and the poisonous lies and flatteries by which he corrupted the kingdom affect all the characters. Rosencrantz and Guildenstern, Hamlet's former friends, agree to spy on him for the king and, finally, although they do not know it, to convey him to his death. Hamlet compares them to poisonous snakes, whom he "will trust as . . . adders fang'd" (III, iv). Ophelia dutifully cooperates with her father's plan to spy on Hamlet, and after Hamlet kills her father, she commits suicide, maddened by "the poison of deep grief" (IV, v). Laertes, corrupted by Claudius's lies and flattery and by "buzzers" who "infect" his "ear with pestilent speeches of his father's death" (IV, v), plots with Claudius to kill Hamlet with a poisoned foil.

Closely associated with the imagery of poison is the imagery of corruption and disease. Claudius says, "my offence is rank, it smells to heaven" (III, iii). After Hamlet commits his own offense of killing Polonius, Claudius calls him a "foul disease" (IV, i); and Hamlet, even before he incurs that guilt, reveals to Guildenstern that his "wit's diseas'd" (III, ii). Although the cause and source of the disease is Claudius, by the end of the third act the sickness has spread to all of Denmark and, in Hamlet's eyes, to the whole world. Prolonged contemplation of evil has infected

Hamlet with a vision of despair, changed him from the "unmatch'd form and feature of blown youth" to a tortured soul "blasted with ecstasy" (III, i). As Hamlet tells Rosencrantz and Guildenstern,

> . . . it goes so heavily with my disposition that this goodly frame, the earth, seems to me a sterile promontory, this most excellent canopy, the air, look you, this brave o'erhanging firmament this majestical roof fretted with golden fire, why, it appears no other thing to me than a foul and pestilent congregation of vapours. What a piece of work is a man! How noble in reason! How infinite in faculty, in form and moving! How like an angel in apprehension! How like a god! The beauty of the world! The paragon of animals! And yet, to me, what is this quintessence of dust?
>
> (II, ii)

Many critics have explained Hamlet's disillusionment psychologically, and Hamlet's own statements, such as "I have of late—but wherefore I know not—lost all my mirth" (II, ii), seem to invite this interpretation. But the corrupted Danish court is not simply a projection of Hamlet's sick imagination. It is, within the play, an objective fact and an analogue of the primal Fall, which was also an objective fact to Shakespeare's audience. Hamlet is undeniably right when he tells Guildenstern, "my wit's diseased" (III, ii), but the source of the disease is clearly identified within the play as Claudius. The spiritual illness in Denmark does not originate with Hamlet, nor is it confined within the boundaries of his soul. The imagery of poison and disease is associated with all the characters, with the entire state, and with nature itself. The behavior of the characters, the disorders in the state, even the bitter winter weather that has inexplicably fallen upon

Denmark a "little month" after the old king was murdered while sleeping in his orchard—all serve to
demonstrate the pervasive effects of Claudius's poison.

Critics have proposed various explanations for Hamlet's failure to take his revenge more quickly, ranging
from the requirements of the revenge play tradition to
Hamlet's own psychological incapacity. Hamlet repeatedly castigates himself for failing to act, most
notably in the soliloquies beginning "O, what a rogue
and peasant slave am I!" (II, ii) and "How all occasions
do inform against me" (IV, iv); and the ghost's final
visitation is, as he tells Hamlet, "to whet thy almost
blunted purpose" (III, iv). And yet, there are a number of good reasons for Hamlet's failure to take his
revenge more directly, and one might even argue that
a quicker, more efficient revenge on Claudius would
have failed to achieve Hamlet's purpose.

When the ghost first reveals the murder, Hamlet
excitedly swears to "sweep" to his revenge "with wings
as swift/As meditation or the thoughts of love" (I, v),
but after his initial excitement subsides, he realizes that
he lacks sufficient evidence to take action against
Claudius. In the first place, he has an educated man's
skepticism about ghosts. When Marcellus tells Horatio
what "some say" and "they say" about the habits of
ghosts (I, i), Horatio replies, "So have I heard and do
in part believe it." After Hamlet speaks with the ghost,
he tells Horatio, "There are more things in heaven
and earth, Horatio,/Than are dreamt of in our philosophy" (I, v). But even though he instinctively accepts
the ghost's revelations, he later decides to test them
before acting; for he knows, he says, "the spirit that I
have seen/May be the devil; and the devil hath power/
T' assume a pleasing shape; yea, and perhaps/Out of
my weakness and my melancholy,/As he is very potent
with such spirits,/Abuses me to damn me" (II, ii).

In distrusting the ghost, Hamlet does what any educated person of Shakespeare's day would have done. Horatio and Marcellus also distrust it, and they try (I, iv) to keep Hamlet from going with it. Contemporary theory on ghosts and spirits held: "True it is that many men do ... persuade themselves that they see or hear ghosts: for that which they imagine they see or hear proceedeth either of melancholy, madness, weakness of the senses, fear, or of some other perturbation."[6]

Hamlet also feels he must test Claudius, for the smiling king has a pleasant, reasonable manner, the court has accepted him, and the ghost's accusations are as outrageous—and as difficult for common sense to accept—as the fact of his appearance. Hamlet's "prophetic soul" is willing to accept the notion that "one may smile, and smile, and be a villain" (I, v), but his reason forces him to distrust his soul's intuition. Hamlet knows that his father's death and his mother's hasty, inappropriate remarriage have plunged him into melancholy. His despairing soliloquy beginning "O, that this too too solid[7] flesh would melt" comes in the second scene of the play, before he has seen the ghost or heard his story. The fact that his "prophetic soul" has suspected his uncle before he hears the ghost's account does not necessarily validate that account; it can serve equally well to discredit it as a product of his own disordered imagination or a demon's attempt to play upon it. Hamlet's motivation for staging his "mousetrap" is, as he tells Horatio, to test himself and the ghost as well as the king: "Observe mine uncle. If his occulted guilt/Do not itself unkennel in one speech,/It is a damned ghost that we have seen,/And my imaginations are as foul/As Vulcan's stithy" (III, ii).

The ghost's injunctions to Hamlet are simple: Revenge the murder, "taint not thy mind," contrive nothing against your mother. Hamlet, however, sees his mission in much more complicated terms. To him, the very "time is out of joint," and his mission is "to set it right" (I, v). He must "catch the conscience of the king" (II, ii) and send his soul to damnation rather than simply slaughtering his body. He keeps his resolve to "speak daggers" to Gertrude "but use none" (III, ii), but his furious insistence that she understand the extent of Claudius's guilt and her own participation in it violates the spirit, and perhaps also the letter, of the ghost's command to "leave her to heaven" and her own conscience.

We see the complexity of Hamlet's mind not only in the tortured philosophical questionings in his soliloquies but also in the ironic wit and sharply observed imagery that characterize even his casual utterances. The first words Hamlet speaks in the play are the bitter puns that demonstrate his appreciation of the more-than-verbal complexity that betrays our attempts to categorize and segregate our experience into neat, rational pigeonholes we can understand and control. His use of homely images reveals a corollary habit of mind; unlike Brutus, who could ignore the irrationality and unpredictability of the Roman mob and of human nature itself, because he conceived his experience in abstract terms, Hamlet notices and remembers the specific. He remembers his father's devotion to his mother not as an abstraction but as a specific act: "so loving to my mother/That he might not beteem the winds of heaven/Visit her face too roughly." He is horrified by her hasty remarriage "within a month . . . /A little month, or e'er those shoes were old/With which she followed my poor father's body." He bitterly remarks to Horatio that "the funeral baked-meats /Did coldly furnish forth the marriage tables" (I, ii). The specificity of Hamlet's imagination prevents him from discounting the evidence of his senses and reducing his experience to manageable abstractions that would enable him to act without further consideration or compunction.

The ghost, in contrast, has the single-minded passion of a pure—or impure—spirit. His simple commands show the difference between his one-dimensional view of Hamlet's mission and Hamlet's own view, which is attended by all the ambivalence that can complicate moral choice for human beings, who must choose and act in an imperfect and ambiguous mortal world. Hamlet wants more than simple revenge; he wants to make sure his mother will repent, rather than leaving her to heaven and her own conscience; he wants to make sure Claudius will be punished in the next world; and, perhaps most of all, he wants to act "in perfect conscience." As late as the second scene of Act V, he asks Horatio,

> He that hath kill'd my king and whor'd my
> mother,
> Popp'd in between th' election and my hopes,
> Thrown out his angle for my proper life,
> And with such cozenage—is't not perfect con-
> science,
> To quit him with this arm? And is't not to be
> damn'd,
> To let this canker of our nature come
> In further evil?

Only at the end of the play does Hamlet submit his will to providence; defying his own premonition about the duel with Laertes, as well as Horatio's warning, he says,

> ... we defy augury. There's a special provi-
> dence in the fall of a sparrow. If it be now, 'tis
> not to come, if it be not to come, it will be
> now; if it be not now, yet it will come; the
> readiness is all.
>
> (V, ii)

But for most of the play, Hamlet's characteristic action is to attempt to know the unknowable and control the uncontrollable. His failure to kill Claudius at prayer lest he "send the villain to heaven" is of a piece with his "To be, or not to be" soliloquy, which attempts to weigh "the heart-ache and the thousand natural shocks/That flesh is heir to" against the unknown perils of "something after death" that will afflict the spirit in "the undiscover'd country from whose bourn/No traveller returns" (III, i). In both cases Hamlet attempts to look beyond the grave, to know what cannot be known and to foresee what cannot be foreseen.

The fatal sword thrust in the dark that kills Polonius and incurs Hamlet's own blood-guilt is ironically appropriate, for Hamlet's fault is his attempt to transcend the limits of mortal vision and act in the prideful assurance of perfect conscience. In a sense then, the bloodbath at the end of the play is as much Hamlet's fault as Claudius's; and the play within the play, in which the criminal is the king's nephew, seems to lend support to this interpretation. And yet, it is important to consider what would have happened if Hamlet had obeyed the ghost's injunctions perfectly, had not doubted the ghost's story or the king's guilt or his own intuitions, had dispatched the king directly, had kept from tainting his mind by prolonged meditation on corruption, and had left his mother to heaven and the stings of her own conscience.

There is little doubt that the holocaust at the end would have been avoided; Hamlet would not have killed Polonius (or Rosencrantz and Guildenstern); Ophelia would not have died, nor would Laertes or Gertrude. And Hamlet would have fulfilled his duty to avenge his father's murder. But Hamlet is not only his father's son; as the play's title tells us, he is also the Prince of Denmark. When he leaps into Ophelia's grave, he cries, "This is I, Hamlet, the Dane!" (V, i), and his royal duty is to purge his corrupted country as well as to avenge his father's murder. When the play opens, Claudius has already poisoned "the whole ear of Denmark" with his lies and flatteries, and he has already drawn the court into unwitting complicity with his crime. The literal poisonings that strew the stage with corpses in the final scene are only a physical analogue to the spiritual corruption that was present all along. The poetic justice of the end was under-scored in one production of the play by having Ham-let, after stabbing the king with Laertes's poisoned foil, slowly and deliberately pour the contents of the poisoned cup into Claudius's ear. And even the tradi-tional staging, in which Hamlet forces the king to drink the poisoned cup, emphasizes Laertes's dying comment that "he is justly serv'd;/It is a poison temp'red by himself." Although Hamlet and Laertes exchange forgiveness before they die, Laertes's death by his own poisoned foil is also, as he admits, just: "The foul practice/Hath turn'd itself on me" (V, ii). And although Gertrude never planned to poison her son, her own death by Claudius's poisoned cup is an ironic parallel to the initial process by which she allowed herself to be corrupted by his flattery. In Sonnet 114 Shakespeare compares flattery, the "mon-arch's plague," to a poisoned cup that he, deluded by infatuation, "drinks" when he allows himself to be deceived. In the last scene of *Hamlet* Gertrude trans-lates the metaphor into literal action.

By the end of the play all the characters who have been symbolically poisoned are dead, most of them by actual poison, and the Danish state is finally purged of Claudius's evil. This purgation, and not simple revenge, is what Hamlet has desired from the first, so there is a very important sense in which he could not have ful-filled his mission by obeying the ghost's injunctions more directly. The holocaust at the end is necessary because all of the victims have been previously corrupted by Claudius, and so all of them will have to die if Hamlet is to cleanse his corrupted country. Of course, one of the victims is Hamlet, for he too has been poisoned, drawn, in thought and act, into the web of deceit and murder that has entangled the Danish court. Significantly, even when Hamlet does finally kill Claudius, it is not until he himself has been fatally poisoned.

Hamlet's two great efforts—the first leading to the play in the third act, the second to the killings at the end—are to make the truth manifest and purge the corrupted consciences and infected souls of his people. But it is only at the end, and only at the cost of blood, that the truth becomes literally manifest; for the "mousetrap" play, like the visitations of the ghost, is a dubious and perhaps delusory apparition. The only time the truth about Claudius and his court becomes literal and public fact is in the final moments of the play when Fortinbras comes in from the outside world to see the carnage and hear Horatio's story.

The critical debate about Hamlet's procrastination is likely to continue. Shakespeare has put Laertes, a headlong revenger, in the play; and Laertes, although he will stop at nothing to get his revenge—even, he says (IV, vii), if he has "to cut his throat in the church"—ends, as Hamlet does, a poisoned poisoner. Some critics have argued that Laertes's fate vindicates Hamlet's action, for it suggests that in Claudius's court the rash as well as the cautious are doomed to the same end. However, it is also possible to argue that if Hamlet had killed Claudius more quickly, Polonius would not have died, and Laertes would have had no need to seek revenge. Yet another conclusion is possible —that the common fate of Hamlet and Laertes is Shakespeare's implicit criticism of the revenge code itself. Ultimately, there seems to be no way of reaching a definitive answer. In spite of all we can say about him, Hamlet remains one of the great enigmas of our literature. His complexity is such that all our critical formulations, if we insist on them as definitive analyses rather than suggesting them as tentative descriptions, seem presumptuous.

The temptation to pluck out the heart of Hamlet's mystery persists, and Freudian critics have been especially industrious in attempting to demonstrate that this play is a kind of case study of a disordered psyche. But their arguments, in addition to oversimplifying one of the greatest of literary characterizations, have the additional fault of denying Hamlet's dramatic context in the guilty Danish court and the fearful relevance by which it reaches out to "catch the conscience" of "guilty creatures sitting at a play." Hamlet tells Gertrude that her efforts to discount his revelations as the utterances of his madness will be nothing but a "flattering unction" to "skin and film the ulcerous place" in her own soul (III, iv). Perhaps there is something equally self-protective in all our efforts to define the character of Hamlet.

Othello, the Moor of Venice

Othello is a very different sort of play from Hamlet. The dramatic structure is clear and simple. The characters are fewer in number and simpler in their motivations. The villain is thoroughly wicked, not a mixed figure like Claudius. The hero is a soldier, a man of action, with none of Hamlet's appetite for contemplation or philosophical speculation. The issues are domestic and personal, not political and cosmic. In fact, one is tempted to speculate that Shakespeare wrote Othello as a kind of foil to Hamlet; for in addition to all these contrasts in structure and characterization, the two plays seem neatly antithetical in their approach to the tragic theme of evil. What destroys Othello is his failure to know: he mistakes Desdemona's goodness and Iago's evil, and he fails to recognize the hidden potentiality for evil within himself until after it has erupted in irrevocable action. What destroys Hamlet is his failure to act: he is so distrustful of appearances and so sensitive to the complexities of his situation and the equally mysterious complexity of his own motives that he fails to kill Claudius until he himself has been poisoned and his own death is inevitable. Hamlet would never have killed Desdemona without testing her innocence and Iago's story. Placed in Hamlet's position, Othello would have killed Claudius in Act II.

Such speculations, however, are finally frivolous. For the position in which each tragic hero is placed is not an accident of life but a dramatic calculation designed to display his character and exercise his potentialities for tragic action and suffering. Placed in Othello's situation, Hamlet would not be a tragic hero, and placed in Hamlet's, neither would Othello. The universe of each tragedy is in part a projection of its hero. But it is also a function of its villain, and, like him, it is designed to serve as a kind of nemesis for the hero. Othello and Hamlet are, each in his own way, preeminently good men, adequate to most things, but tragically inadequate to survive the one situation in which their enemies—and their playwright—place them.

Iago's activity in *Othello* has been compared to that of the playwright, for it is he who controls the action; and, like a tragic playwright, he takes artistic delight in the subtlety and skill with which he contrives the hero's ruin. In many productions of the play, Iago's role seems to overshadow Othello's, and critical discussions tend to center on the question of Iago's motivation more than Othello's.

It is Iago and not Othello who repeatedly reveals his thoughts in soliloquy, but in spite—or perhaps because—of all the reasons he gives for his actions, his motivation remains problematic. The first and simplest explanation Iago gives is what he tells Roderigo in the opening scene: Othello passed him over for promotion and made Cassio his lieutenant instead. But then in a soliloquy at the end of Act I Iago says he suspects that Othello has cuckolded him, and in another soliloquy at the end of the following scene, he repeats this explanation and adds two more: he loves Desdemona, although "not out of absolute lust," and he suspects that Cassio, as well as Othello, has made him a cuckold.

This proliferation of motives suggests that Iago is not so much revealing reasons for his actions as constructing rationalizations to explain them. At the very end of the play, when Othello wants to "demand that demi-devil [Iago]/Why he hath thus ensnar'd my soul and body," Iago replies:

> Demand me nothing; what you know, you
> know.
> From this time forth I never will speak word.
> (V, ii)

And even in his soliloquies Iago never declares a specific motive sufficient to account for the extent of his malice.

There is some evidence that Iago does not fully understand his own motivation. When he says in his first soliloquy, "I hate the Moor;/And it is thought abroad that 'twixt my sheets/He has done my office," the order of the two clauses suggests that his hatred is prior to his suspicion, and the "and" that joins them fails to establish any causal relationship between the two. His second soliloquy implies, by the disorder of its construction, that Iago is groping for explanations of an enmity he feels but cannot himself understand, and the final lines of both speeches can refer to Iago's motives as well as his plans, both of which he seems to be making up as he goes along. The first soliloquy concludes:

> I have't. It is engend'red. Hell and night
> Must bring this monstrous birth to the world's
> light.
> (I, iii)

And the second ends even more tentatively:

> 'Tis here, but yet confus'd;
> Knavery's plain face is never seen till us'd.
>
> (II, i)

Iago's motives, like his plans, seem to originate in an infernal region whose depths even he cannot fathom.

Iago's failure to provide a satisfactory motive for his villainies has led many critics to adopt Coleridge's view that they stem from "a motiveless malignity" and to seek for explanations in Iago's character. In the first scene, Iago implies his absolute antipathy to all that Othello represents ("were I the Moor, I would not be Iago") and his hatred for all loyal servants ("whip me such honest knaves"). The "daily beauty" that Cassio displays in his life makes Iago wish him dead (V, i). Iago's often-quoted comment to Desdemona, "I am nothing if not critical" (II, i), suggests that there is a metaphysical dimension to his subversive, negative spirit, as does his comment in the opening scene, "I am not what I am," which inverts the biblical identification of God, "I am that I am."

Iago's devotion to evil is so absolute that it supports metaphysical and theological interpretations of his character. It also associates him with the conventional Elizabethan dramatic figure of the Machiavellian villain, but Iago is an intensified Machiavel. The Machiavel's traditional atheism becomes in Iago a skepticism of all goodness, human as well as divine. The Machiavel's traditional opportunism becomes Iago's compulsion to do evil for its own sake, and not merely as a means of benefiting himself. Othello's idealism and his innocent confidence in the power of his "perfect soul" (I, ii) make him Iago's natural victim, for Iago's motivation is not so much personal and particular as diabolical and general.

Iago repeatedly associates himself with hell and devils. He tells Roderigo, "If sanctimony and a frail vow betwixt an erring barbarian and a super-subtle Venetian be not too hard for my wits and all the tribe of hell, thou shalt enjoy her" (I, iii). He says in his first soliloquy, "Hell and night/Must bring this monstrous birth to the world's light" (I, iii). Contemplating his own hypocrisy, he remarks, "When devils will the blackest sins put on,/They do suggest at first with heavenly shows,/As I do now" (II, iii). Cassio identifies the "invisible spirit of wine" with which Iago has made him drunk as a "devil" and his behavior in the drunken brawl Iago instigated as the work of the "devil wrath" (II, iii). Othello, maddened by the jealousy Iago has inspired in him, cries, "fire and brimstone!" (IV, i). And at the end of the play, before he attempts to kill Iago, he wonders whether Iago has cloven hoofs:

> I look down towards his feet; but that's a fable.
> If that thou be'st a devil, I cannot kill thee.

Iago replies, "I bleed, sir; but not kill'd" (V, ii).

Because of all these allusions, it is tempting to reduce Iago to a kind of allegorical figure, a devil from the old morality plays transported to Shakespeare's secular theater. But although he is unequivocally evil, Iago is a character and not simply a personification of the abstract quality of wickedness. For one thing, Iago is the victim of his own subversive spirit and not simply its unmoved mover. When Emilia first learns of Othello's jealousy, she does not know that Iago has incited it, but she says, "The Moor's abus'd by some most villainous knave," and "Some such squire he was/That turn'd your wit the seamy side without,/And made you to suspect me with the Moor" (IV, ii). The audience, having seen the development of Iago's jealousy in his first two soliloquies, knows she is right.

In the first soliloquy Iago says, "I know not if 't be true;/But I, for mere suspicion in that kind,/Will do as if for surety" (I, iii). By the end of the following scene his jealousy has grown so strong that the mere thought of it "doth," he says, "like a poisonous mineral, gnaw my inwards" (II, i). There is no evidence anywhere in the play that Iago's jealousy has any external foundation. Instead, his own testimony, as well as Emilia's intuition, suggests that it was created out of nothing by the same diabolical spirit that destroyed Othello's faith in Desdemona.

Iago's character is further defined by his language. He frequently uses animal images, often of loathsome small creatures preying on each other. A loyal servant, Iago says, is "like his master's ass." A sincere man is like one who wears his "heart upon [his] sleeve/For daws to peck at." He tells Roderigo to "plague" Othello "with flies." He tells Brabantio, "Even now, now, very now, an old black ram/Is tupping your white ewe," and warns him, "you'll have your daughter cover'd with a Barbary horse; you'll have your nephews neigh to you; you'll have coursers for cousins, and gennets for germans." "Your daughter and the Moor," he says, are "making the beast with two backs" (I, i). The fact that Iago uses these images to describe human beings engaged in virtuous, and even idealized, actions helps to define his evil as a depraved habit of mind and soul, a quintessential subversiveness, an obsessive need to reduce humanity and the ideals to which it aspires to a base and bestial condition.

Iago's speech patterns reveal the same habit of mind. Music, and musical verse, were associated in Shakespeare's time with cosmic order and with its earthly analogues in ordered communities and human love. Iago's affinity for chaos is expressed in the broken, unrhythmical verse he uses as well as in his thoughts and actions.

At the beginning of the play Othello speaks in terms and forms that directly contrast with Iago's.[8] Instead of hell and devils, he speaks (in I, iii) of "heaven," "prayer," "pilgrimage," "faith," "pity," "redemption," and "love." Instead of the beasts and insects that make up the lower links in the chain of being, Othello speaks of the moon, the sea, the hills, and the heavens. Instead of disordered congeries· of confused thoughts, his speeches are orderly, and his characteristic poetry is regular and mellifluous blank verse. Instead of colloquial and even vulgar language, he uses elevated and abstract diction. Listening to Othello speak, Desdemona fell in love with him; for, she says, "I saw Othello's visage in his mind" (I, iii). The language he uses, no less than the tales he tells, expresses the noble habit of mind that won Desdemona and, just as inexorably, made Iago his enemy.

Othello's language changes, however, during the course of the play. As Iago gradually destroys his faith in Desdemona, he also destroys Othello's noble vision of himself and of the world, and Othello gradually adopts the language of Iago's despairing cynicism. When Iago first hints that Desdemona is unfaithful, Othello tries to resist the stirrings of jealousy, but his language shows that he has already begun to think in Iago's terms: "Exchange me for a goat/When I shall turn the business of my soul/To such ... surmises" (III, iii). After pressing his insinuations further, Iago leaves Othello to an unhappy soliloquy in which the bestial terms he uses indicate how much he has already fallen under Iago's spell:

> If I do prove her haggard,
> Though that her jesses were my dear heart-
>   strings,
> I'd whistle her off and let her down the wind
> To prey at fortune. . . .

Othello (Paul Robeson) and Iago (José Ferrer) swear
vengeance on Cassio and Desdemona (III, iii) in Margaret
Webster's 1943 Theatre Guild Production at the Shubert
Theatre, New York.

> . . . .
> . . . I had rather be a toad
> And live upon the vapour of a dungeon
> Than keep a corner in the thing I love
> For others' uses.

As Iago recognizes, "the Moor already changes with my poison," and in the rest of the scene (III, iii), Othello uses more and more of Iago's language: "cords," "knives," "poison," "fire," "suffocating streams," "death and damnation," "goats," monkeys," "wolves," "aspics' tongues," "hate," "hell," "damn." Later, after he and Iago swear their wicked pact to kill Cassio and Desdemona, Othello disintegrates utterly. His speech becomes completely disjointed:

> Lie with her! lie on her! We say lie on her, when they belie her. Lie with her! 'Zounds, that's fulsome!—Handkerchief—confessions—handkerchief! To confess, and be hang'd for his labour;—first to be hang'd, and then to confess. . . . Pish! Noses, ears, and lips.—Is't possible?—Confess—handkerchief!—O devil!
> (IV, i)

And he falls in a wordless trance.

Before Iago began his poisonous insinuations, Othello prophetically described the significance of his love for Desdemona:

> Perdition catch my soul,
> But I do love thee! and when I love thee not,
> Chaos is come again.
> (III, iii)

The language he uses after Iago destroys that love gives the audience a glimpse of the chaos into which he has fallen. In destroying Othello's faith in Desdemona, Iago destroys the very principle of order in Othello's universe. "If she be false," says Othello, "then heaven mocks itself!" (III, iii). Once Iago convinces him that she is false, Othello cannot believe in cosmic order or even maintain the sense of his own nobility that produced his proud bearing and soaring poetry. He now belongs to Iago and shares Iago's absolute faithlessness.

Desdemona's point of view is not greatly developed in the play; she is important chiefly for what she means to Othello and the other characters. But the symbolic imagery they associate with her establishes her as an antithesis to Iago: to all who speak of her, she embodies positive values, and to the more perceptive she is associated with the principles of order, love, holiness, and harmony. Brabantio calls her a "jewel" (I, iii). Cassio calls her the "riches of the ship" that brings her to Cyprus, and he also calls her "divine" (II, i). Even Roderigo knows "she's full of most bless'd condition" (II, i). Desdemona is an idealized character, and Othello's love for her is an expression of his own idealism.

Othello's love is so idealized that it discounts physical appetite. He wants Desdemona to come to Cyprus, he says, "not/To please the palate of my appetite,/ Nor to comply with heat... /But to be free and bounteous to her mind" (I, iii). Opposed to this idealized love is Iago's cynicism, which would reduce it to lustful appetite:

> These Moors are changeable in their wills...
> the food that to him now is as luscious as
> locusts, shall be to him shortly as bitter as
> coloquintida. She must change for youth; when
> she is sated with his body, she will find the
> error of her choice.... If sanctimony and a
> frail vow betwixt an erring barbarian and a
> super-subtle Venetian be not too hard for my

> wits and all the tribe of hell, thou [Roderigo]
> shalt enjoy her.
>
> (I, iii)

As usual, Iago is lying: Desdemona is incapable of lust or faithlessness, and Roderigo will not enjoy her. But there is a germ of truth in what he says, for Othello and Desdemona have had vastly different lives and have been accustomed to vastly different manners, and Iago can exploit these differences to arouse Othello's suspicions and to prevent Desdemona from allaying them. Desdemona, obviously, does not know Othello any better than he knows her. She falls in love with the romantic hero of the tales he told Brabantio—in other words, with Othello's poetry and his own idealized conception of himself. Her ineffectual efforts to dispel Othello's jealous suspicions and rage show her lack of familiarity with his moods and manners. Like Othello, she has fallen in love with an ideal, and like him, she is fatally ignorant of the person who embodies that ideal. In Act II, scene i, when she is waiting anxiously to see if Othello's ship has survived the tempest and landed safely on Cyprus, she passes the time in sophisticated badinage with Iago. The audience knows her anxiety, for she stops to ask about the ships, and she says, "I am not merry; but I do beguile/The thing I am by seeming otherwise." Those same sophisticated Venetian manners, which also appear in her attempts to soothe Othello's terrible rage by gentle remonstrations and urbane bearing, are tragically inappropriate to her new milieu. Cyprus is a military camp, and Othello's experience has been dominated by extravagant adventures and great wars, where good and evil, and friend and enemy, are sharply distinct. He has served the Venetian state as a soldier, but he has remained an alien to the subleties of Venetian manners.

Nonetheless, in the end. Iago is wrong. Desdemona's love survives the ultimate test, and Othello recognizes her worth and loves her again before he dies. If his innocent idealism makes him vulnerable to Iago's attacks, it also permits him a nobility of vision that Iago can never achieve. Iago tells Roderigo (II, i), "they say, base men being in love have then a nobility in their natures more than is native to them." Iago, who cannot love, is equally incapable of nobility; he can only report—no doubt skeptically—what "they say" about the mysterious workings of those alien qualities. Iago wields the formidable powers of hell in the play, but Desdemona represents the influence of love, which seems to prevail at the end.

Ulysses' famous speech on "degree" (the principle of civic and cosmic order) in *Troilus and Cressida* helps to explain Desdemona's significance. Describing the chaos that ensues when degree is broken, Ulysses says, "Take but degree away, untune that string,/And, hark, what discord follows" (I, iii). He goes on to describe a state of universal strife, concluding, "This chaos, when degree is suffocate,/Follows the choking." Desdemona, who represents the principle of order in Othello's universe, is, like the principle of order Ulysses describes, associated with music, and Iago, the agent of chaos, is opposed to it. When Othello and Desdemona meet on Cyprus, Othello kisses her and says, "And this, and this, the greatest discords be/That e'er our hearts shall make!" (II, i). Iago's aside, "O, you are well tun'd now!/But I'll set down the pegs that make this music,/As honest as I am," helps to define his role as a destroyer of harmony. But Desdemona sings a sweet sad song of unrequited love when she prepares for bed for the last time, and even Emilia, Iago's own wife, dies, as she says, "in music," speaking the truth and singing Desdemona's song (V, ii). Moreover, before the end of the play Othello recovers his own gift of musical language, and with it his vision of an ordered, noble universe. Iago manages to beguile all of them and cause their deaths, but he cannot, finally, untune the string of harmony or imprison the other characters in the infernal chaos of his own imagination.

Just before he kills Desdemona, Othello resumes the beautiful poetry and celestial imagery he used at the beginning of the play:

> It is the cause, it is the cause, my soul,—
> Let me not name it to you, you chaste stars!—
> It is the cause. Yet I'll not shed her blood,
> Nor scar that whiter skin of hers than snow,
> And smooth as monumental alabaster.
>
> (V, ii)

He speaks of "light," a "rose," a "heavenly" sorrow, and "love." This is the language of Othello's idealism; although he is about to "suffocate" and "choke" Desdemona, his words show that he will do the killing in the name of the ideal order she represented and not as an agent of Iago's chaos.

Although Othello kills Desdemona in the last scene of the play, his language changes twice more before the end. After he learns that Desdemona was true, he falls into despair again and cries,

> Whip me, ye devils,
> From the possession of this heavenly sight!
> Blow me about in winds! roast me in sulphur!
> Wash me in steep-down gulfs of liquid fire!
> O Desdemon! dead, Desdemon! dead!
> Oh! Oh!

Then in his final speech, just before he kills himself, Othello returns again to the beautiful poetry and exotic imagery of his idealism:

Soft you; a word or two before you go.
I have done the state some service, and they
    know 't.
No more of that. I pray you, in your letters,
When you shall these unlucky deeds relate,
Speak of me as I am; nothing extenuate,
Nor set down aught in malice. Then must you
    speak
Of one that lov'd not wisely but too well;
Of one not easily jealous, but, being wrought,
Perplex'd in the extreme; of one whose hand,
Like the base Indian,[9] threw a pearl away
Richer than all his tribe; of one whose subdu'd
    eyes,
Albeit unused to the melting mood,
Drops tears as fast as the Arabian trees
Their medicinal gum. Set you down this;
And say besides, that in Aleppo once,
Where a malignant and a turban'd Turk
Beat a Venetian and traduc'd the state,
I took by th' throat the circumcised dog,
And smote him—thus.

Critical responses to Othello's final speech range from appreciation of its beautiful pathos to arguments that it exhibits self-deluded sentimentality. Did Othello love "too well" or not well enough? Was he "not easily jealous" or pathologically so? Does his allusion to the pearl show that he, like Brabantio, regarded Desdemona as a mere possession, or does it show his recognition of her true worth. Or is the "pearl" a reference to his own immortal soul? These and other questions about the speech are unlikely to receive definitive answers, and critics continue to make persuasive arguments for widely varying interpretations.

There seems to be little doubt, however, that Othello does not die in Iago's power, for whatever the limitations of his own perceptions and code of values as we saw them at the beginning of the play, he seems now to recapture the poetic eloquence that bespoke them. When he lost his faith in Desdemona, he also lost the ordering principle that sustained his vision of himself and of the universe. By the beginning of Act V, scene ii, however, Othello manages to reassemble his shattered cosmos, to regain his faith in heaven and justice and in himself as their agent, with Desdemona now redefined as a deceptively beautiful object of righteous sacrifice. "She must die," he decides, "else she'll betray more men." He speaks of heaven and of his love for Desdemona even as he prepares to kill her. He grieves for her death in lines that describe the destruction of cosmic order but retain the characteristics of linguistic order that are native to Othello's own vision and alien to Iago's: "Methinks it should be now a huge eclipse/Of sun and moon, and that th' affrighted globe/Did yawn at alteration." When Emilia tries to tell him Desdemona was true, he says, "Had she been true,/If Heaven would make me such another world/Of one entire and perfect chrysolite,/I'd not have sold her for it" (V, ii). But when Emilia finally convinces him of his error, Othello's perfect universe falls apart again. Now it is he who is cast out into infernal chaos and Desdemona who remains in heaven ("when we shall meet at compt,/This look of thine will hurl my soul from heaven,/And fiends will snatch at it"), and he is again overcome by a despairing vision of hell.

The recovery suggested by the eloquent language of Othello's final speech is more difficult to explain, but it may be that the closing image provides a clue. Othello speaks of two figures—a malignant Turk who traduced the Venetian state and bore the mark of an infidel's religion and himself, the faithful and righteous warrior who killed the Turk. And he enacts both parts when he kills himself. Othello has been limited throughout to a simplistic warrior's vision of the world, which divided people into the righteous and the unrighteous, the friend and the enemy, and which could not deal with human complexity. His idealized vision of himself and his need to idealize all his experience demanded that Desdemona be either angel or strumpet, that hate was the only alternative to love and killing the only expression of hate. When Iago first made him suspect Desdemona, Othello demanded "ocular proof," for he could not tolerate uncertainty ("to be once in doubt/Is once to be resolv'd. . . ./I'll see before I doubt; when I doubt, prove;/And on the proof, there is no more but this,—/Away at once with love or jealousy!" III, iii). This simplicity of vision made Othello vulnerable to Iago's machinations; and once they succeeded, Othello exchanged his simplistic idealism for Iago's equally absolute—and equally incomplete—pessimism. Othello finally managed, in the scene in Desdemona's bedchamber, to sustain his faith in an ordered universe even without believing in Desdemona's virtue, but he could no longer sustain it after Emilia's revelation destroyed his faith in his own righteousness. Like Iago, he despaired of his own salvation and suffered a vision of universal disorder and evil. At the end of the play, however, Othello is finally able to recognize his own guilt (for the Turkish infidel, who has been his enemy in war and an analogue to Iago in the play, is Othello) and still retain and act upon his vision of an ordered universe (for the faithful soldier who kills the Turk is also Othello).

If this reading of Othello's last speech is correct, then Othello has finally surpassed Iago in understanding as well as nobility. Iago had seemed from the first to be much cleverer than his noble but simple-minded general, but his vision was just as limited as Othello's. He could not understand Othello's ideals or do good any more than Othello could understand the intricacies

of Iago's wickedness. Othello saw a simplified universe
defined by grand ideals, with himself as the noble protagonist of heroic adventures. Iago saw an equally
partial vision of a chaotic universe filled with pred-
atory beasts driven by their appetites. He knew his
own depravity and its external counterparts, and he
managed to make Othello share his pessimism and for-
get his own nobility and idealism. But in the end,
Othello is able to see his own guilt and still retain his
faith in external order—a double vision that Iago never
achieves. Iago has glimpses of goodness, but he cannot
sustain them in the face of his own despair. When
Desdemona asks him, "What would'st thou write of
me, if thou shouldst praise me?", he seems momen-
tarily reluctant to apply his corrosive wit to her goodness. "O gentle lady," he says, "do not put me to't;/
For I am nothing if not critical" (II, i). But she
persists, and Iago replies, as he must, in the pessimistic
terms of his despair.

The one time that Iago speaks in Othello's grandil-
oquent language is at the end of Act III, scene iii, after
Othello, swearing to kill Cassio, commits himself to
Iago's power:

> Witness, you ever-burning light above,
> You elements that clip us round about,
> Witness that here Iago doth give up
> The execution of his wit, hands, heart,
> To wrong'd Othello's service!

It might be argued that Iago here uses Othello's language in a calculated effort to appeal to Othello's idealism,
for Othello has just called his oath of vengeance a
"sacred vow." But it is also possible to see in this
episode the consummation for which Iago has been
reaching. Othello's idealism has attracted Iago as inexorably as the innocence of Adam and Eve attracted

Satan. He is drawn to Othello even as he hates him, just as he admits in soliloquy that he loves Desdemona and "not out of absolute lust" even while he plots her destruction. Both lovers inhabit an Edenic world from which Iago is debarred by his despair, and he longs for it even while he is driven to attack it. There is bitter irony in the final words in this scene, when after swearing to kill Cassio and Desdemona, Othello says to Iago, "Now art thou my lieutenant," and Iago replies, "I am your own forever." Swearing to kill both his faithful friend and his loyal wife, Othello has actually committed himself to Iago's service. But there is another implication too, a suggestion of Iago's moral and psychological dependence upon Othello.

It is sometimes argued that *Othello* is a melodramatic play and that its hero is merely pathetic, that it lacks the ethical sophistication and the grandeur of Shakespeare's greatest tragedies. However, its simplicities can be seen as necessary embodiments of its theme. Just as *Hamlet* can be seen as a play organized around the theme of poison, with all the symbolic implications that poison carries as a secret and insidious form of evil, *Othello* can be seen as a play about black and white. Although Othello's character, like his speech, suffers violent changes during the course of the play, these changes are all from one extreme to another, not the subtle shifts in mood and point of view that define Hamlet's progress. The whole play, like Othello's imagination, is conceived in terms of great antitheses— good and evil, black and white, heaven and hell, love and warfare, Venice and Cyprus, friend and foe. But although the play does contain melodramatic elements, it is not finally or simply a melodrama but rather a tragedy that explores the moral implications of a melodramatic vision of human experience.

King Lear

King Lear has been called the greatest of Shakespeare's tragedies and the most difficult, but the characterization is remarkably simple. Most of the characters are clearly "good" or clearly "bad"; and the virtues distinguishing the good are neatly balanced by corresponding vices in the wicked. The good are loyal. Banished, Kent returns in disguise to serve his king. Disinherited, Cordelia returns to fight and die for her father. The Fool pines for Cordelia when she goes to France and remains with his king through the horrors of the storm. Edgar, although proclaimed an outlaw by his father, Gloucester, becomes his father's guide and protector when Gloucester is himself outlawed.

The wicked are disloyal. Goneril, to whom Lear gave everything, betrays him. But her disloyalty does not stop there. As Albany warns her:

Portions of this chapter originally appeared in my article "Delusion as Resolution in *King Lear*," *Shakespeare Quarterly*, Winter, 1970, pp. 29–34, and are reprinted here by permission.

That nature which contemns its origin
Cannot be bordered certain in itself.
She that herself will sliver and disbranch
From her material sap, perforce must wither
And come to deadly use.

(IV, ii)

Having violated the bond between father and child, having betrayed her husband and murdered her sister, her deadly treachery finally exhausts its external objects and she kills herself. Regan and Cornwall betray the man who is at the same time king, father, and benefactor, then proceed to violate the bond between guest and host when they blind Gloucester and turn him out of his own house. Edmund begins by betraying his brother, proceeds to betray his father, then plots with Goneril against Albany, and finally gives orders for Cordelia's murder in prison. The treachery of the wicked characters is as prodigious as the loyalty of the good.

Another neat antithesis between the two sets of characters lies in their opposing views of nature. Edmund's soliloquy at the beginning of the second scene presents in its most explicit form the viewpoint of the evil characters. Declaring that "Nature" is his goddess, he defines the "law" of nature as the law of might, whose only standards are wit and strength and cunning. Edmund's creed is the law of the jungle that informs the letter he forges—the law that finds "an idle and fond [that is, foolish] bondage in the oppression of aged tyranny; who sways, not as it hath power, but as it is suffer'd" (I, ii).

To Edmund bastardy is a more "natural" kind of birth than legitimacy. This judgment accords with the modern usuage of the term "natural son" to mean "bastard." In Shakespeare's time, the term "natural son" could have at least three meanings. First, there was the modern meaning—a son born out of wedlock. Second, there was a meaning that has been obsolete since the eighteenth century—a son born *in* wedlock. And third, there is a meaning we have retained, although it has lost some of its force—a son who feels the "natural" affection and loyalty that a child *should* feel toward a parent. When Gloucester, responding to Edmund's seemingly loyal opposition to Edgar, says, "Loyal and natural boy, I'll work the means/To make thee capable" (II, i), he is using "natural" in the third sense and probably in the second as well—meanings that are absolutely precluded by Edmund's concept of "Nature." To Edmund, the rites and norms of society and the bonds of love and duty are the mere "plague of custom," the "curiosity of nations." To Gloucester, they define the natural state of human life.

When the good characters call Goneril's and Regan's treatment of their father "unnatural," they are not speaking in terms of Edmund's "Nature" but of its opposite: they imply that what is "natural" to human beings is not the bare minimum—the strength and cunning that we share with the beasts—but is the highest possibility of civilization and duty, which is embodied in human society and moral law. The sentiments that Edmund falsely attributes to Edgar when he says (I, ii), "I have heard him oft maintain it to be fit that, sons at perfect age and fathers declin'd, the father should be as ward to the son, and the son manage his revenue" (I, ii), accord perfectly with Edmund's view of Nature. Gloucester, who holds an antithetical view, calls those sentiments "unnatural."

The evil characters tend to rely, as Lear himself does in the opening scene, upon a quantitative standard of value. Lear repudiates Cordelia because "nothing will come of nothing" (I, i). To the King of France, however, Cordelia is "most rich being poor,/Most choice forsaken, and most lov'd despis'd," an "unpriz'd precious maid" (I, i). Cordelia also rejects the quantitative standard; when she returns to fight for her father, she tells him she has "no cause" to do him wrong (IV, vii). Ignoring rational calculation, her loyalty is directly opposed to the disloyalty of her sisters, who rationalize their behavior in terms of measurable "need."

In the horrifying scene in which Goneril and Regan strip Lear of his followers—and, with them, his dignity —they repeatedly invoke the standard of "need." At the beginning of the scene Regan tells Lear to return to Goneril and ask her forgiveness. Lear responds with bitter irony:

> Ask her forgiveness?
> Do you but mark how this becomes the house:
> "Dear daughter, I confess that I am old;
> Age is unnecessary. On my knees I beg
> That you'll vouchsafe me raiment, bed, and food."
>
> (II, iv)

As the scene progresses, Regan tells Lear that fifty followers should be enough for him: "What should you need of more?" The next logical step, and Regan's next comment, is "Yea, or so many?" A minute later she tells Lear that he can bring no more than twenty-five. Lear, still thinking in quantitative terms himself, turns to Goneril:

> I'll go with thee.
> Thy fifty yet doth double five and twenty,
> And thou art twice her love.

Goneril responds:

> Hear me, my lord:
> What need you five and twenty, ten, or five,
> To follow in a house where twice so many
> Have a command to tend you?

And Regan completes the process of reducing Lear to "nothing" with "What need one?" At this point, Lear finally seems to learn:

> O, reason not the need! Our basest beggars
> Are in the poorest thing superfluous.
> Allow not nature more than nature needs,
> Man's life is cheap as beast's.

The final product of quantitative measurement, of "reasoning" the "need," is the same as the final product of Edmund's concept of nature and of the repudiation of loyalty as a standard of behavior: a human life becomes as cheap as a beast's.

The ideal of society implied by the actions and values of the good characters is hierarchical, a society characterized by loyalty, duty, and cohesiveness; a society animated by values that transcend reason and measurement. The opposing concept of society is, perhaps, in Elizabethan terms no society at all, but it is familiar today. It is individualistic and atomistic. There is no duty higher than self-aggrandizement and no standard of value but quantitative measurement—or price.

And yet the play is not simply an apology for a traditional, hierarchical society. The generalizations I have made, like almost any generalization one attempts to make about *King Lear*, are not completely accurate. I have said that the good characters are distinguished by their loyalty and the evil ones by their disloyalty, but there are two important cases where this is not so. After Cornwall has put out one of Gloucester's eyes, a servant of Cornwall's stands up and kills his master. Clearly, this is an instance of good disloyalty. Similarly, Oswald, who is thoroughly wicked, is "a serviceable villain,/As duteous to the vices of [his] mistress as badness would desire" (IV, vi). Thus, it seems that loyalty is not enough to justify or disloyalty enough to condemn an action in the universe of this play. And in fact this ambivalence goes beyond these individual cases to characterize the hierarchical society itself.

The ambivalence is most apparent in the clothing symbolism, which plays an important part in this play in the form of metaphors and allusions as well as in costume changes that mark the stages in a character's progress. After Lear tells Goneril, "Allow not nature more than nature needs,/Man's life is cheap as beast's," he goes on to explain, "Thou art a lady;/If only to go warm were gorgeous,/Why, nature needs not what thou gorgeous wear'st,/Which scarcely keeps thee warm" (II, iv). Here and throughout the play, clothing is associated with the social hierarchy, with an individual's place in society and with the traditions that govern social behavior. Nakedness is associated with the danger of being thrust outside the social framework, of being brought to the condition of a beast, of being reduced to "nothing."

The Fool tells Lear that when he divested himself of his kingship, his place in society, he became "nothing." He describes Lear's abdication as a literal undressing— giving away his crown and putting down his breeches (I, iv). When Edgar is outlawed, he removes his clothing to become Tom o' Bedlam. He says he will "take the basest and most poorest shape/That ever penury, in contempt of man,/Brought near to beast. . . ./And with presented nakedness out-face the winds and persecutions of the sky" (II, iii). He goes on to describe the life he expects as a Bedlam beggar, harried from town to town and from farm to farm, and concludes, "Edgar I nothing am."

Clothing, then, like society, is necessary to human life, even if not to animal survival, for it serves to define a person's social identity and thus to ward off the onslaughts of human evil as well as the "persecu-

Mary Hara and Patricia Hamilton as Goneril and Regan in the American Shakespeare Festival Theatre's 1965 production of *King Lear*, directed by Allen Fletcher. The clothes symbolism loses much of its significance in many modern productions of *King Lear*, in which the characters are dressed in rough, heavy garments appropriate to the pre-Christian setting of the Lear story. In this production, for example, in Act II, scene iv, Goneril and Regan are muffled in floor-length cloaks with hoods—obviously warm and not at all gorgeous.
AMERICAN SHAKESPEARE FESTIVAL THEATRE, STRATFORD, CONN.

tions" of nonhuman nature. And yet, clothing can also be evil. The villainous Oswald is completely a thing of clothes. Kent tells Oswald that a tailor made him, and to emphasize the line, Shakespeare has Kent repeat it for Cornwall: "Nature disclaims in thee," he says. "A tailor made thee" (II, ii). Clothing, like the society it symbolizes, serves to protect and enhance the value of human life, but it can exact a heavy price from its wearers. It can be a disguise as well as a protection. After he has lost his own "clothing," Lear cries out against the evil that hides beneath the orderly surface of society and the "clothes" that conceal it:

> Thou rascal beadle, hold thy bloody hand!
> Why dost thou lash that whore? Strip thy
> own back;
> Thou hotly lusts to use her in that kind
> For which thou whip'st her. The usurer hangs
> the cozener.
> Through tatter'd clothes great vices do appear;
> Robes and furr'd gowns hide all. Plate sins
> with gold,
> And the strong lance of justice hurtless breaks;
> Arm it in rags, a pigmy's straw doth pierce it.
>   (IV, vi)

Lear finishes, ludicrously but significantly, by calling for his own boots to be pulled off.

Lear does not learn pity until he has been stripped and exposed to the storm. Contemplating the sufferings of the "poor naked wretches" who must endure such storms unprotected, Lear associates clothing with houses and both with the protections that social rank provides:

> Poor naked wretches, wheresoe'er you are,
> That bide the pelting of this pitiless storm,
> How shall your houseless heads and unfed
> sides,
> Your loop'd and window'd raggedness, defend
> you
> From seasons such as these?
>   (III, iv)

Here, Lear recognizes the dangers of nakedness and, by implication, the value of clothing. But he goes on to say:

> O, I have ta'en
> Too little care of this! Take physic, pomp;
> Expose thyself to feel what wretches feel,
> That thou mayst shake the superflux to them,
> And show the heavens more just.

Lear's clothing—his place at the top of the social hierarchy—has kept him from seeing the injustice in his society.

The clothing symbolism, in keeping with the complex and paradoxical universe of *King Lear*, is radically ambivalent. To be stripped of one's clothes is to become "nothing," a "poor, bare, forked animal" defenseless against whatever pitiless storm may come. But if clothes are the only means of distinguishing people from animals, they do not provide a very clear distinction. Lear says to the naked Edgar:

> Thou ow'st the worm no silk, the beast no hide, the sheep no wool, the cat no perfume. ... Thou art the thing itself; unaccommodated man is no more but such a poor, bare, forked animal as thou art.
>
> (III, iv)

The clothes that make the man are "lendings" from the beasts.

In Act I, scene i, the clothes are on. Lear is the absolute monarch, protected by all the trappings his society can afford. And he is blind. Kent tells him, "see better, Lear," but Lear refuses to heed him. Regan is probably right when she says at the end of the scene that Lear "hath ever but slenderly known himself." For as Lear later recognizes, his life as a king has kept him from knowledge of his true condition:

> They flatter'd me like a dog, and told me I
> had the white hairs in my beard ere the black
> ones were there. To say "ay" and "no" to
> everything that I said! ... When the rain came
> to wet me once, and the wind to make me
> chatter; when the thunder would not peace at
> my bidding; there I found 'em, there I smelt
> 'em out. Go to, they are not men o' their
> words: they told me I was everything; 'tis a
> lie, I am not ague-proof.
>
> (IV, vi)

Lear gains knowledge only after he loses his splendid royal clothing and crown. Paradoxically, however, the knowledge Lear gains is a recognition of the very things that make clothes necessary and nakedness dangerous: the continuing existence of evil in the natural world and in the human heart, and the defenselessness of an unclothed creature against its storms.

Lear is stripped of everything—even of his reason. And reason is closely associated with clothing in *King Lear*. When Edgar becomes an outlaw and removes his clothes, the role he assumes is that of a madman. The Fool tells Lear (I, iv) that when he stripped himself of the breeches that made him a man and the crown that made him a king, he became a fool: "All thy other titles thou hast given away; that thou wast born with." Later in the play, when he is mad, Lear tells Gloucester, "When we are born, we cry that we are come/To this great stage of fools" (IV, vi). Reason, like all the other attributes by which human beings distinguish themselves from the beasts, is thus defined as an acquisition and not a birthright; it is, in other words, a form of clothing and shares its ambivalent status.

Like the other forms of clothing, reason seems, ironically, to obscure important truths, for once Lear is mad, he asks the ultimate questions about human life. Seeing the naked Edgar disguised as Tom o' Bedlam, Lear asks, "Is man no more than this?" Later in the same scene (III, iv) he asks, "What is the cause of thunder?"— a question that does more than demonstrate that Lear has lost his wits, since it also questions the reason for all the calamities that are visited upon human beings by the physical universe. He might just as well have asked the cause of earthquakes, of plagues, and of the deaths of innocent children. The implications are the same. Lear's third question (III, vi) is a demand to know what causes the evil within the human heart: "Then let them anatomize Regan; see what breeds about her heart. Is there any cause in nature that make these hard hearts?"

Lear is not the only character who asks such questions. Difficult theological questions are constantly being raised in the play, and by it as well. Before the final battle, Edgar tells Gloucester to "pray that the right will thrive." His words still ring hollowly in our ears when we learn, almost immediately, that Cordelia's forces have been defeated (V, ii). After Edmund confesses that he and Goneril have given orders that Cordelia be murdered, Albany says, "The gods defend her!" No sooner has he spoken than Lear enters with Cordelia's corpse in his arms (V, iii). Gloucester, having been blinded by Regan and Cornwall and told that his trusted son Edmund betrayed him, says (IV, i), "As flies to wanton boys, are we to th' gods,/They kill us for their sport." Yet Albany, hearing of the same event, fixes upon the fact that Cornwall was killed while committing the crime and decides (IV, ii) that "this shows you are above,/You justicers, that these our nether crimes/So speedily can venge!" To Kent and Gloucester, it is "the stars above us" that "govern our conditions" (IV, iii). To Edmund and Edgar, such a belief is foolish. Shakespeare seems in *King Lear* to confront every possible thesis about the action and its implications with an antithesis but never to allow a synthesis to emerge.

The very complexity of the issues raised in *King Lear* seems almost to preclude their resolution. Any attempt to resolve into unity the extremes of hope and despair, of virtue and vice, depicted in *King Lear* must satisfy an audience that has seen too much by the end of the play to accept either the easy "poetic" justice of a happy ending or the perhaps equally easy pessimism that would deny justice entirely. As a result, any attempt at resolution runs a tremendous risk of looking false. Shakespeare solves this problem, I think, by presenting the resolutions *as* false, at least from certain angles of vision; and the result—his dramatic representation—looks wonderfully true.

Shakespeare has Edgar perpetrate delusions—or play practical jokes, but very serious ones—on other characters; and these jokes (or delusions or deceptions) serve to resolve a number of major issues in the play. Edgar's deceptions contain important elements of truth, but they never fully lose their delusory quality. The first of Edgar's deceptions, and the most memorable, is the one by which he persuades Gloucester that he has been saved from death by a miracle. Having led his blinded father to a flat place near Dover, Edgar persuades him that he is at the top of a high cliff. The audience sees that the stage is flat and knows that it represents a flat field. But Edgar persuades Gloucester that it is the high cliff he sought in order to commit suicide. Edgar "trifle[s] thus with his despair/...to cure it" (IV, vi), for Gloucester's sufferings have made him lose faith in the goodness of the gods and the order of the universe. After Gloucester leaps, Edgar tells him in a changed voice that he has been miraculously saved from a great fall and from an evil spirit who led him to the cliff:

> It was some fiend; therefore, thou happy father,
> Think that the clearest gods, who make them honours
> Of men's impossibilities, have preserv'd thee.
>
> (IV, vi)

What Edgar says is literally a lie but symbolically perfectly true. Gloucester *has* fallen from a tremendous height, he *has* been led by an evil spirit (as he himself acknowledges later in the scene: "You ever-gentle gods, take my breath from me;/Let not my worser spirit tempt me again/To die before you please!"), and he has been saved by a miracle—the miraculous devotion of the son he cruelly and unjustly repudiated. The man-made "miracle" by which Edgar saves Gloucester seems to be the only kind of miracle possible in the universe of this play, in which the ordinary relationship between people and gods appears to be reversed. When Lear plans the life of renunciation he hopes to share with Cordelia in prison, he says, "Upon such sacrifices, my Cordelia,/The gods themselves throw incense" (V, iii), inverting the customary relationship in which the people, the worshipers, would throw the incense upon the sacrifice. The same inversion is even more explicit when Lear cries in the tempest:

> Take physic, pomp;
> Expose thyself to feel what wretches feel,
> That thou mayst shake the superflux to them,
> And show the heavens more just.
>
> (III, iv)

In each case, the status of the gods and of the heavens is determined by the actions of people on earth. The "visible spirits" that Albany hopes the heavens will send down to punish the guilty (IV, iii) never appear, and the only justice we see in *King Lear* is a human creation.

Edgar creates his second illusion of justice when he kills Oswald. Meanly dressed, Edgar speaks in a rustic dialect to reinforce Oswald's impression that he is a peasant, and then he kills Oswald with a cudgel, a peasant's weapon. Oswald's fault throughout has been that he is completely the creature of the social and political hierarchy, unaware of any values beyond worldly status or any code beyond manners. So completely and so merely the creature of the hierarchy that he serves as a perfect embodiment of its deficiencies, Oswald is nothing but clothes, and therefore inhuman. If the poor, bare, forked animal that Lear beholds in the storm needs clothes to distinguish him from the beasts, the thing made by a tailor lacks even the natural affections that distinguish the beasts from inanimate things (as Kent recognizes when he tells Oswald, "Nature disclaims in thee"). Even the opportunism that makes Edmund brutal and enables him to betray his own father seems to lack the sheer deadliness of the pragmatism with which Oswald responds to the sight of poor, blind Gloucester:

> A proclaim'd prize! Most happy!
> That eyeless head of thine was first fram'd flesh
> To raise my fortunes. Thou old unhappy traitor,
> Briefly thyself remember; the sword is out
> That must destroy thee.
>
> (IV, vi)

Oswald sees a human being as a "prize." He reduces the whole purpose of Gloucester's existence to "raising" Oswald's "fortunes." Gloucester, to Oswald, is an economic advantage, pure and simple.

In view of Oswald's inability to distinguish value from rank, the justice of his death at the hands of a peasant, a person of no rank at all—is very neat. The fact that the peasant is Edgar, dressed in rough clothes and speaking a rustic dialect, complicates the justice and reconciles it to the infinitely complex universe of *King Lear*. Although Oswald dies believing he was killed by a "slave," the audience knows that Edgar is really the eldest son of an earl. The "justice" of Oswald's death is thus inextricably mixed with delusion. And even the fact of Oswald's delusion contains an element of justice. Goneril's snobbish minion has never understood the human nobility that high social rank was supposed to embody, and at his death he is literally ignorant of Edgar's noble rank.

The third of Edgar's deceptions is in many ways the opposite of the second, and in creating it Edgar assumes a shape exactly opposite to his previous one. Dressed in the knightly trappings that befit his station but concealing his identity, Edgar challenges Edmund to fight and kills him. Again the manner is perfectly appropriate. For if Oswald is too much the creature of society, Edmund is too much its adversary. Edmund's first major speech proclaimed his defiance of the "curiosity of nations" and the "plague of custom." And it is these things that, in the end, cut him down in the person of his despised, legitimate older brother, dressed in armor and fighting in formal knightly combat. Like Oswald, Edmund is finally destroyed by a representative of all the values he has defied and ignored; and in both cases the representation is, at least from one point of view, a deception.

Edmund's final act is an attempt to do "some good ... despite" his "own nature" (V, iii). He reveals that he has given orders for Cordelia to be hanged and urges Albany to save her. Edmund's attempt to do good is in "despite" of his "own nature" in two ways. First, there is Edmund's own evil disposition, of which he is perfectly aware:

> My father compounded with my mother under the dragon's tail, and my nativity was under *Ursa major;* so that it follows, I am rough and lecherous. Fut, I should have been that I am, had the maidenliest star in the firmament twinkled on my bastardizing.
>
> (I, ii)

Edmund's dying attempt to do good is "in despite" not only of the evil nature he knows he has but also of the "goddess" to whom he declared his allegiance, the "Nature" who knows no right but the brute strength and ruthless cunning that enable one animal to win out over another. Edmund's vision of her law, like his disposition, was incapable of providing a basis for a genuinely good act. And yet, Edmund does not really refute what he has said before, either about his own disposition or about the universe, for he does not say that his nature has changed, or that his Nature is different from what he thought it was. In fact, his statement that he is acting in "despite" of it implies logically that it has not changed. To be sure, Edmund has qualified the picture he gave previously of his "own nature" (or Nature), for that picture lacked the means to account for a good deed. Without denying the truth of what he has said before, he has simply gone on to behave differently.

At the end of the play, as at the beginning, the two views of nature coexist: the antithesis fails to eliminate the thesis, but instead seems to entail it. Nowhere is this ambiguity more apparent than in the conclusion of the play. Shakespeare's sources reunited Lear and Cordelia for a happy ending. His late-seventeenth-century reviser, Nahum Tate, even included a marriage between Edgar and Cordelia. Today, Shakespeare's ending is generally conceded to be effective, but there is widespread disagreement about its meaning. Lear's dying words—"Do you see this? Look on her, look, her lips,/Look there, look there!" (V, iii)—bring the questions to a head. What does Lear see, or think he sees? Is Cordelia meant to be living or dead? And if she is dead, is she merely dead, or does Lear somehow "see" that her soul still lives?

Critical interpretations of the speech run the gamut from a mystical vision of divine grace to a horrified realization of utter chaos. To A. C. Bradley, "any actor is false to the text who does not attempt to express, in Lear's last accents and gestures and look, an unbearable *joy*," for Lear "is sure, at last, that she *lives*" even though the audience knows "he is deceived."[10] To J. Stampfer, in contrast, "there is no mitigation in Lear's death, hence no mitigation in the ending of the play." The aesthetic unity of the play demands that Lear's heart must "burst in the purest agony at his eternal separation from Cordelia." The play depicts a "universe in which even those who have fully repented, done penance, and risen to the tender regard of sainthood can be hunted down, driven insane, and killed by the most agonizing extremes of passion."[11] And, at the opposite extreme, Harold C. Goddard sees in the speech a demonstration "that there is a mode of seeing as much higher than physical eyesight as physical eyesight is than touch, an insight that bestows power to see 'things invisible to mortal sight' as certainly as Lear saw that Cordelia lives after death."[12]

As these differing interpretations indicate, the immediate questions raised by Lear's final speech—what does Lear see, and how true is his vision?—lead, fairly directly, to the much larger questions raised by the play as a whole: "Is man no more than this?" "What is the cause of thunder?" "Is there any cause in nature that make these hard hearts?" Are we to the gods "as flies to wanton boys"? Are there just gods above us who speedily punish our crimes? Do the stars really "govern our conditions"?

One reason why Lear's last words are so difficult to interpret is that the passage itself seems to support an optimistic reading, while the play as a whole seems to demand a pessimistic one. The speech begins in despair and in a vision of nature as a meaningless chaos:

> And my poor fool is hang'd! No, no, no life!
> Why should a dog, a horse, a rat, have life,
> And thou no breath at all? Thou'lt come no
>   more,
> Never, never, never, never, never!
>
> (V, iii)

At this point, when despair is total, there is a transition. Lear turns to someone to ask, "Pray you, undo this button" (whether the button is his or Cordelia's is the subject of debate), and to respond, "thank you, sir." When he turns his attention back to Cordelia in the next two lines, he seems to be seeing something new that he had not seen before:

> Do you see this? Look on her, look, her lips,
> Look there, look there!

And yet the first four lines of the speech left nothing new in the way of despair for Lear to perceive. The only new thing he could be seeing, it would seem, is some grounds for hope. It is to her lips that he has looked for hope earlier in the scene, when he called for a looking glass to see if her breath would mist it, when he held a feather up to her lips to see if it would move, and when he imagined she had spoken. All of this tends to suggest that what he now sees on her lips is grounds for hope, whether real or imaginary, but as the many arguments to the contrary attest, the implication is by no means certain.

In fact, the ambiguity of Lear's final speech is very much like the ambiguity of Edgar's deceptions. In each case, Edgar deceives other characters, and the audience knows they are deceived. And in each case, the deceptions take the form of delusions of justice in an apparently unjust or meaningless universe. Although Oswald dies as he lived, a "serviceable villain," his death is as near as we come in *King Lear* to poetic justice. And Gloucester and Edmund are clearly changed by Edgar's deceptions, which seem to carry a kind of saving grace as they cure Gloucester's despair and prepare the way for Edmund's extraordinary end.

In Lear's case, we cannot even be sure that he is deluded, and whatever delusion there is is apparently self-imposed; but it is still instructive to compare his final speech with the delusions Edgar creates and with Lear's own behavior in the opening scene of the play. In the opening scene, Lear required conclusive evidence from Cordelia's lips that she loved him, and when she was unable to provide it, he repudiated her. Lear, like Edmund, "has come full circle" by the end of the play: again he is looking to Cordelia's lips for evidence, but this time he is willing to believe without it. The audience has no evidence other than Lear's word that Cordelia is anything but dead and that the universe of the play is anything but a meaningless chaos in which a dog, a horse, a rat have life and a Cordelia no breath at all. But the very lack of evidence, the very difficulty of belief, is what serves, paradoxically, to make Lear's belief so meaningful.

Lear has just said that if Cordelia lives, "It is a chance which does redeem all sorrows/That ever I have felt." But at this point the audience has seen too much of Lear's world to regard such a "chance" as anything more than a random, and finally meaningless, piece of good luck. After Lear dies, Kent rebukes Edgar for trying to revive him:

> Vex not his ghost. O, let him pass! He hates
> him
> That would upon the rack of this tough world
> Stretch him out longer.

There has, by now, been far too much evidence that this is a "tough world" for one chance to convince the audience of the existence of an external, benevolent Providence intervening in human life. Lear would probably be convinced that Providence had intervened and satisfied that all his sorrows had been "redeemed," for now Cordelia is all that matters to him. But Lear matters to the audience, and if Cordelia did live, the contingency of his faith upon a fortuitous occurrence, a mere "chance," would surely lessen in their eyes the meaning of his death. For as it stands, Lear's death is meaningful. It is meaningful, and even triumphant, because his final assertion of faith, like Edgar's deceptions and Edmund's dying attempt to do some good in despite of his own nature, is "something" that has come of "nothing" in defiance of the rational, quantitative standard of measurement that made Lear repudiate Cordelia in the opening scene. In seeing something on Cordelia's dead lips, Lear finds his own redemptive illusion to oppose the universal destruction he unleashed when he failed to see Cordelia's love because she could not "heave [her] heart into her mouth" (I, i).

In *King Lear* it is the very absoluteness of the evil that gives force and meaning to the human actions that defy evil. In Act IV a gentleman tells Lear, "Thou hast one daughter/Who redeems nature from the general curse/Which twain have brought her to" (IV, vi). At the end Cordelia and Lear die, and the general curse on nature seems to remain, but it does not finally prevail against the redemptive power of the goodness and love that Cordelia still represents.

Macbeth

Macbeth has dramatic antecedents in the tragedies of Christopher Marlowe, who organized simple—and even episodic—plots around the crimes of a titanic protagonist who dominated the action and fascinated the audience by his poetic eloquence and his outrageous career. Shakespeare wrote his own Marlovian tragedy early, in *Richard III*, but it was not until *Macbeth* that he transformed Marlowe's formula into a richly complicated study of damnation in all its psychological complexity and metaphysical horror.

Unlike *Hamlet* and *King Lear*, *Macbeth* contains no subplots, and the main plot is remarkably simple. The complexity of the play derives from its complicated language, themes, and characterization. Unlike Lear or Othello, Macbeth is profoundly introspective and subject to powerful internal conflicts between opposed motives and values. His soliloquies reveal those conflicts in language so richly allusive and so elliptical that it often verges on opacity, for despite all his anguished questionings, Macbeth cannot fully understand the nature of his crimes until after he has committed them.

Macbeth is a study in the occult process of damnation, defined as the play progresses in complex, symbolic actions that embody the same themes as the language. One of the most important of these themes is time. *Macbeth* is the shortest of Shakespeare's tragedies and one of his shortest plays. Many scholars have argued that the text we have is an abridgment, but there is good reason to believe Shakespeare intended the play to be short, for Macbeth's action is repeatedly characterized as a race against time, and the brevity of the play helps to reinforce this effect. References to time permeate the language of the play, and the concept of time, in one or another of its permutations, seems to be involved with all the other major symbols.

The play opens with a question about time—"When shall we three meet again . . . ?"—and an answer—"ere the set of the sun"—that symbolically foreshadows what will happen. In Shakespeare's day the king was traditionally associated with the sun, and sunset was a typical image for his death or overthrow. It also symbolizes a loss of reason; for reason, the intellectual light that illuminates our thinking, is the sun's analogue on the level of the microcosm, the individual human psyche, just as the king is its analogue on the level of the macrocosm, the state. The sunset thus adumbrates Macbeth's crime—the killing of the king—and the irrational state of mind in which he will conceive it, execute it, and suffer its effects. In addition, sunset suggests the milieu of the play, for the entire action will take place in darkness—the internal darkness in which Macbeth conceives his crimes, the literal darkness in which he commits them, and the symbolic darkness his reign brings down on all of Scotland. Finally, sunset suggests an obilteration of time. Time is measured by the sun, and the irrationality and disorder associated with night are also associated with the obliteration of regular temporal sequence.

At the close of the play, when Macduff announces that he has killed Macbeth, he also says, "The time is free" (V, viii). Macbeth's reign of evil has stopped time in an unnatural, unending night, but now the time is free to resume its natural, orderly course. Taking over the ravaged kingdom, Malcolm announces that he will perform all needful acts "by the grace of Grace/ ... in measure, time, and place" (V, viii). Both phrases are equally important: Malcolm will rule by divine grace to redeem his country from Macbeth's satanic dominion, and he will act "in measure, time, and place" to restore the order that Macbeth's unnatural defiance of time has disrupted. Even Malcolm's language contrasts with Macbeth's characteristically tortuous constructions and disjointed rhythms in its lucidity, its measured, harmonious rhythms, and its rational, sequential order.

At the beginning, when the witches tell Macbeth he will "be King hereafter," he tries to quell the "horrid image" their prophecy immediately suggests to his guilty imagination by reminding himself, "If chance will have me King, why, chance may crown me/ Without my stir" and "Come what come may,/ Time and the hour runs through the roughest day" (I, iii). But his infected imagination keeps him from obeying his own good advice to let time take its natural course.

Because Macbeth is unable to wait for the orderly process of time to bring in the future, because he cannot wait for time to accomplish the event the witches promised him "hereafter," he kills Duncan to bring the future into the present. Lady Macbeth, whose rapport with her husband is so close that she seems almost to be a projection from his own psyche, tells Macbeth:

> Thy letters have transported me beyond
> This ignorant present, and I feel now
> The future in the instant.

(I, v)

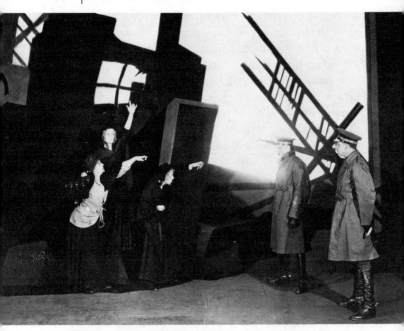

Sir Barry Jackson, in his 1928 production of *Macbeth* performed by the Birmingham Repertory Theatre at the Royal Court Theatre in London, updated the action of the play to the period of World War I. In Act I, scene iii, Eric Maturin as Macbeth and Marshall Sheppard as Banquo meet the three witches (Muriel Aked, Joan Pereira, and Una O'Connor).

Like Macbeth, she wants to outrace time and seize the future, and like him, she will suffer later the effects of what she does now. After the murder she tells Macbeth, "a little water clears us of this deed," and she dismisses the anguished cry he says he heard that "Glamis hath murder'd sleep, and therefore Cawdor/ Shall sleep no more; Macbeth shall sleep no more" as a "brainsickly" delusion (II, ii). But at the end of the play it is she who is "brainsick," walking and talking in her sleep, obsessively washing the hands that she now knows will "ne'er be clean," for "all the perfumes of Arabia will not sweeten" one of them (V, i). Moreover, she reenacts the crime in disordered time sequence—first the blood, then the preliminaries to the murder, then the blood again—in an endless, disjointed, and repetitive recitation of the horrors that will end only with her own death. And after she dies, Macbeth will protest, "She should have died hereafter" (V, v), ironically repudiating her desire—and his own—at the beginning of the play to bring the "hereafter" promised by witches into the present.

An image repeatedly associated with Macbeth at the beginning of the play is that of a racer on horseback. Duncan expresses his gratitude for Macbeth's past loyalty in terms that ironically describe his impending treachery: "Thou art so far before/That swiftest wing of recompense is slow/To overtake thee" (I, iv). Macbeth races to his castle to get there ahead of Duncan so that he and Lady Macbeth can plan their coming guest's murder; and when Duncan arrives, he again praises Macbeth as a swift racer, making the same mistake he made before by ascribing Macbeth's speed, ironically, to love and duty: "We cours'd him at the heels, and had a purpose/To be his purveyor; but he rides well,/And his great love, sharp as his spur, hath holp him/To his home before us" (I, vi).

The irony is intensified when, a minute later, the next scene begins with Macbeth in soliloquy, contemplating Duncan's murder, and using the same image of himself as a racer on horseback. Attributing his speed to "ambition" rather than "love," he equates his evil attempt to murder Duncan with the horse that will carry him to his destination: "I have no spur/To prick the sides of my intent, but only/Vaulting ambition, which o'erleaps itself/And falls on th' other" (I, vii). Later in the play, when he hears that Macduff has fled to England, Macbeth is afraid time is beginning to outrace him:

> Time, thou anticipat'st my dread exploits:
> The flighty purpose never is o'ertook
> Unless the deed go with it. From this moment
> The very firstlings of my heart shall be
> The firstlings of my hand.
>
> (IV, ii)

Trying to close the temporal gap between purpose and action, he orders the immediate murder of Macduff's wife and children, and all others "that trace him in his line"—to destroy, in effect, Macduff's future by obliterating his line of descendants.

An essential premise of tragedy is that acts—especially criminal acts—have consequences, that effect follows from cause in inexorable sequence whether or not the actor understands, or even knows, what he has done. Macbeth's special horror is that he knows, before he ever commits his tragic crime, what he is about to do and that he fears, before he ever experiences them, the unknown consequences of his deed. The broken rhythms and obscure, elliptical imagery of his soliloquy at the beginning of Act I, scene vii, betray the disorder and agitation of his thinking, but the speech also indicates that he recognizes the enormity of the deed he contemplates:

> If it were done when 'tis done, then 'twere well
> It were done quickly. If the assassination
> Could trammel up the consequence, and catch
> With his surcease success; that but this blow
> Might be the be-all and the end-all here,
> But here, upon this bank and shoal of time,
> We'd jump the life to come. But in these cases

We still have judgement here, that we but teach
Bloody instructions, which, being taught,
    return
To plague th' inventor.

Macbeth foresees here that the deed will not be "done
when 'tis done," that it will be no "end-all" but instead
a beginning, that what it will begin is an inevitable,
even if unforeseeable, process of tragic consequences
in the future, and that from the moment he kills Duncan, time will be his enemy.

Macbeth does not have time to complete his soliloquy: Lady Macbeth interrupts it and convinces him to
go through with the murder, and at the end of the
scene Macbeth declares his resolve and enjoins his wife
to "mock the time with fairest show" to conceal their
evil purpose. In resolving to kill Duncan, Macbeth has
also to "mock time"; and, in return, time will mock
him. The hypocritical speeches he makes after Duncan's murder ironically describe his situation better
than he knows, for they describe a spiritual condition
that Macbeth has already entered even though he will
not recognize it until the end of the play. Announcing
his murder of Duncan's grooms, Macbeth says, "the
expedition [that is, haste] of my violent love/Outrun
the pauser, reason" (II, iii). Although he is lying about
his love, Macbeth is right when he says his expedition
has outrun his reason, for human reason cannot work
without the temporal basis Macbeth has destroyed, and
his own reason will fail him in the end when he trusts
the equivocal prophecies of the three apparitions.

Macbeth also speaks more truly than he knows when
he says after Duncan's murder:

Had I but died an hour before this chance,
I had liv'd a blessed time; for from this instant,
There's nothing serious in mortality.

> All is but toys; renown and grace is dead;
> The wine of life is drawn, and the mere lees
> Is left this vault to brag of.
>
> (II, iii)

The smooth rhythms, abstract terms, and conventional imagery—all the easy eloquence—of this speech betray its hypocrisy; but the statement is prophetic, for even though he does not yet know it, Macbeth's time is in fact now cursed. It is not until the end of the play, however, when Lady Macbeth dies, that he realizes the truth of the false words he spoke to "mock the time" when Duncan was murdered, and now he repeats his statement, this time in broken rhythms and confused imagery that contrast with the smooth language of his false professions of grief for Duncan and make it an anguished expression of real despair:

> To-morrow, and to-morrow, and to-morrow
> Creeps in this petty pace from day to day
> To the last syllable of recorded time;
> And all our yesterdays have lighted fools
> The way to dusty death. Out, out, brief candle!
> Life's but a walking shadow, a poor player
> That struts and frets his hour upon the stage
> And then is heard no more. It is a tale
> Told by an idiot, full of sound and fury,
> Signifying nothing.
>
> (V, v)

Macbeth's suffering is horribly appropriate: in killing Duncan, he mocked the time and tried to outrace it; in the end time slows down for him to a petty pace that makes life itself a mockery.

Darkness, another major symbol in the play, is obviously related to time. Act II, like Act I, begins with a question about time—Banquo's "How goest the night, boy?"—and an ambiguous answer involving darkness

—"The moon is down, I have not heard the clock." But here the sun has already gone down, and the night has already set in. In Act I, scene v, when Macbeth tells his Lady that Duncan plans to leave their castle "to-morrow," she replies, "O never/Shall sun that morrow see," and her words prove literally prophetic. After the murder Ross remarks that "by th' clock 'tis day,/And yet dark night strangles the travelling lamp" and wonders why "darkness does the face of earth entomb,/When living light should kiss it" (II, iv). An old man responds, " 'Tis unnatural,/Even like the deed that's done." Images of darkness and night play a major role in defining the horror of Macbeth's Scotland. As Ross's "living light" and "entomb" suggest, they stand for death; but they stand not only for the literal murders that Macbeth commits but also, as the old man indicates, for the death of the life principle in nature.

The sun is an analogue for the king, but it is also a fertility principle, and in killing the king Macbeth has transformed the kingdom into a sunless, sterile wasteland, like the "blasted heath" upon which he first met the weird sisters. Just before the murder, Macbeth describes the night in terms that will shortly apply to the entire kingdom: "Now o'er the one half-world/ Nature seems dead, and wicked dreams abuse/The curtain'd sleep. Witchcraft celebrates/... and wither'd Murder/... towards his design/Moves like a ghost" (II, i). Banquo mistrusts the witches from the beginning, calling them "instruments of darkness." In killing the king, Macbeth too becomes an "instrument of darkness," and under his reign Scotland becomes a sunless wasteland where "nature seems dead."

The porter scene, immediately following the murder, further defines the implications of Macbeth's crime. Pretending to be a "devil-porter" at the gate of hell, the porter says he "had thought to have let in some

of all professions that go the primrose way to th' everlasting bonfire" (II, iii). What actually happens after
he opens the gate is that hell comes out to establish
its dark reign throughout the kingdom. "Hell," as
Lady Macbeth will say in her agony (V, i), "is murky"
(and the devil is the prince of darkness). References
to hell abound in the play, and Macbeth is repeatedly
described by epithets like "fiend" and "hell-bound"
and "devilish." In direct antithesis to a rightful king,
who rules by the grace of God and serves as God's instrument in the kingdom, Macbeth becomes the devil's
viceroy and places the kingdom under the devil's
power.

England, by contrast, is ruled by a rightful king, as
the scenes there between Malcolm and Macduff indicate. Earlier critics tended to dismiss these scenes as
Shakespeare's compliment to James I, who, like the
good English king in Shakespeare's play, engaged in
the practice of "touching for the king's evil" (scrofula,
supposedly, was healed by the royal touch). Modern
critics, however, have pointed out that the English
scenes have serious thematic significance and that they
serve to indicate the turning point in the action. When
Macduff first arrives, he and Malcolm are suspicious
of each other, for Macduff has just come from a country infected by the wickedness of the tyrant who rules
it. To test Macduff, Malcolm accuses himself of a
wickedness so great that, he says, when it is known,
"black Macbeth/Will seem as pure as snow," and he
claims that if he is crowned, he will commit every
imaginable crime, "pour the sweet milk of concord
into hell,/Uproar the universal peace, confound/All
unity on earth" (IV, iii). Finally convinced by these
false self-accusations, Macduff, mourning anew for his
poor country and for the loss of the "sainted king"
Duncan, turns to leave Malcolm. But now Malcolm's
own "black scruples" (that is, suspicions) are resolved,

and he formally abjures each of the crimes he has falsely confessed.

Macduff is confused, but at that moment an English doctor enters, and he and Malcolm explain to Macduff the English king's custom of touching for a disease that is "call'd the evil." The English king's supernatural powers of goodness and healing are thus directly opposed to the supernatural powers of evil and infection that Macbeth wields in Scotland. And when Macduff and Malcolm lead their English soldiers back to Scotland to defeat the tyrant, the supernatural forces of good will flow back into the country along with them, just as the suspicion and deceit with which they first respond to each other is an emanation of the evil that flows out of Scotland with them. Significantly, there are two doctors in the play: the English doctor who testifies to the power of a supernatural good beyond the reach of his art, and the Scottish doctor who appears in the following scene (V, i) and says that he is powerless to cure the spiritual evil that has infected Lady Macbeth.

In allying himself with the witches as instruments of darkness, Macbeth has chosen a realm in which reason and knowledge cannot operate, for these powers that illuminate thought are associated with light, and Macbeth has chosen darkness. When he first contemplates killing Duncan, Macbeth says:

> Stars, hide your fires;
> Let not light see my black and deep desires;
> The eye wink at the hand; yet let that be
> Which the eye fears, when it is done, to see.
> (I, iv)

Lady Macbeth calls upon the "sightless substances" of "murd'ring ministers" to steel her for the deed, and she invokes "thick night" palled in "the dunnest smoke of hell,/That my keen knife see not the wound it makes,/Nor heaven peep through the blanket of the dark/To cry, 'Hold, hold!' " (I, v). After he kills Duncan, Macbeth is afraid even "to think what I have done," and he dares not "look on't again" (II, ii). And as he plans to kill Banquo, he begs "seeling night" to "scarf up the tender eye of pitiful day" (III, ii).

To kill Duncan, Macbeth had to "outrun the pauser, reason," and enter the dark world òf the witches, who do a "deed without a name". (IV, i), and like them, Macbeth has done the unspeakable and the unthinkable. There is, in fact, a sense in which Macbeth cannot know what he has done, let alone say it. "To know my deed," he says, " 'twere best not know myself" (II, ii). When Macbeth submits to the power of evil, he loses himself in a dark world of negation in which "nothing is but what is not" and the light of reason will no longer work. When Banquo first sees the witches, he is afraid he has "eaten on the insane root/ That takes the reason prisoner" (I, iii). To murder Duncan, Macbeth must leave the known sunlit world of reason and nature and enter the dark "half-world" of the witches where bloody apparitions beguile the eyes and equivocal words deceive the mind.

As Macbeth knows from the beginning, the crime against Duncan is also a crime against nature. The first "horrid image" of the temptation is, Macbeth says, sufficient "to make my seated heart knock at my ribs,/ Against the use of nature" (I, iii). To Lady Macbeth, it is her husband's "nature/ . . . too full o' th' milk of human kindness" (I, v) that may keep him from killing Duncan; and to fix her own resolution she invokes evil spirits to "stop up th' access and passage to remorse,/That no compunctious visitings of nature/ Shake my fell purpose." The old man in Act II, scene iv, calls the murder "unnatural," and Macbeth himself compares Duncan's wounds to a "breach in nature."

Before he kills Duncan, Macbeth retains enough of a stake in nature to call the deed unnatural and to mistrust the witches' words and his vision of the bloody dagger, even as he is driven to follow their promptings. But once he has done the deed, he seems to expect, ironically, that the old laws of nature will prevail and protect him, even though he has become an agent of the unnatural forces the witches represent. The witches seem to be women, but they have beards. They "look not like th' inhabitants o' th' earth" (I, iii). They have supernatural powers to foretell the future. They speak in paradoxes—"Fair is foul and foul is fair" (I, i)—that invert natural categories. And yet with all this, Macbeth seems to expect that his reason will guide him and that time and nature will follow their accustomed course even after he has allied himself with the witches.

Seeing Banquo's ghost, Macbeth protests pathetically:

> The time has been,
> That, when the brains were out, the man
>   would die,
> And there an end; but now they rise again.
> With twenty mortal murders on their crowns,
> And push us from our stools.
>
> (III, iv)

His trust in equivocal prophecies—that "none of woman born/Shall harm Macbeth" and "Macbeth shall never vanquish'd be until/Great Birnam wood to high Dunsinane hill/Shall come against him" (IV, i)—implies the same irony, for it rests upon rational expectation about the orderly processes of nature. He declares confidently:

> That will never be.
> Who can impress the forest, bid the tree

Unfix his earth-bound root? Sweet bode-
ments! good!
Rebellion's head, rise never till the wood
Of Birnam rise, and our high-plac'd Macbeth
Shall live the lease of nature, pay his breath
To time and mortal custom.

(IV, i)

But Macbeth has violated both nature and time, and
now they rise up to destroy him. Malcolm, Duncan's
natural successor, orders his soldiers to conceal their
numbers by carrying boughs from Birnam Wood, thus
using natural means to accomplish the witches' unnatural prophecy. Like Macbeth earlier, Malcolm must
screen what he is doing, but instead of the darkness
that symbolizes evil and death, he uses the green
boughs that symbolize Scotland's restoration to the
world of life and nature. It is also appropriate that
Macduff, who was "untimely ripp'd" from his mother's
womb, should kill Macbeth. Macduff's birth—untimely
ripped, but to life and not to death—like Malcolm's
ruse, serves symbolically to reestablish the rule of nature in Scotland, just as his killing Macbeth, along with
Malcolm's victory over Macbeth's army, serves literally
to reestablish the rule of a good king. In both cases,
natural events reverse the implications of an unnatural
prophecy.

The apparition of the bloody babe refers most directly to Macduff's birth, but it refers also to Macbeth's murders, and it helps to define the nature of his
guilt. In his desperate attempts to outrace time and
control the future, Macbeth repeatedly attempts to kill
children—real children as well as symbolic ones—and
the language and action of the play, like the hands of
the murderers, are spattered with blood. Contemplating Duncan's murder, Macbeth is afraid that "pity,
like a naked new-born babe/ . . . /Shall blow the horrid
deed in every eye" (I, vii). A few minutes later Lady

Macbeth urges him, in effect, to kill the babe and go through with the murder:

> I have given suck and know
> How tender 'tis to love the babe that milks me;
> I would, while it was smiling in my face,
> Have pluck'd my nipple from his boneless gums
> And dash'd the brains out, had I so sworn as you
> Have done to this.

It is ironically appropriate that Duncan's murder brings Macbeth only a "fruitless crown" and "barren sceptre" and that he futilely attempts to avert the prophecy by ordering the murder of a real child, Banquo's son Fleance. And, in what is probably the most horrifying scene in the play, the audience sees Macduff's child murdered. Macbeth's obscene violations of life and nature have already been depicted in the symbolic imagery of the play, but they are made shockingly visible here. Learning of the deed, Macduff cries, "He has no children" (IV, iii), a remark that probably refers to Macbeth, and not, as some critics have argued, to Malcolm; for it expresses at once Macbeth's punishment—his exclusion from the generative sequence of natural life in time—and the crime for which he incurs it—the failure of pity that transforms him into a kind of archetype of Murder.

The babes Macbeth is willing to kill—the babe that symbolizes pity and the real children who lie in the way of his ambitions—represent life and nature, but they also represent the future. The witches' third apparition, a child crowned, signifies that the children of Duncan and Banquo will be kings, and the procession of eight kings that follows is clearly a procession in time. The crowned child carries a tree in his hand, which, in addition to literally foretelling Malcolm's arrival at Dunsinane, suggests the connection between time and nature that is implicit in the symbol of the child. Banquo asked the witches, "If you can look into the seeds of time,/And say which grain will grow and which will not,/Speak then to me, who neither beg nor fear/Your favours nor your hate" (I, iii). Duncan told Macbeth, "I have begun to plant thee, and will labour/To make thee full of growing" (I, iv). At the end of the play, Malcolm describes the tasks ahead of him as "what's more to do/Which would be planted newly with the time" (V, viii). For the good characters, time is the medium of natural growth, and their own function—planting, cultivation, and nurture—is subject to time's orderly progression. In direct antithesis to Macbeth, they are agents of life, and life on earth proceeds, like Malcolm, "by the grace of Grace/... in measure, time, and place."

At the end of Act IV, when he and Macduff are ready to march on Scotland, Malcolm tells Macduff, "The night is long that never finds the day"; and at the end of the play, when Malcolm prepares to ascend the long-usurped throne, we know that the day has finally returned to Scotland. But most of *Macbeth* takes place in the dark, and despite its brevity, the total effect of the play distorts time in a long nightmare of blood, irrationality, unnatural occurrence, fear, and evil. At the very end Malcolm restores Scotland—and the audience—to the world of the living, but Malcolm's role is relatively slight. Most of the play is dominated by Macbeth, and, through him, by the dark forces that make him their victim and agent in an unearthly world of death and damnation.

Antony and Cleopatra

Antony and Cleopatra is one of Shake-speare's most difficult plays. The language—with its mixed metaphors, elliptical constructions, and violent juxtapositions of elevated diction and coarse slang—is often obscure and sometimes almost incomprehensible. Like the Egyptian queen who is its heroine, the play's language is a curious and often bewildering mixture of the sublime and the vulgar, which defies convention, baffles the reason, and suspends the ordinary categories of thought. Scholars have pointed out that the style in *Antony and Cleopatra* typifies Shakespeare's practice in his late plays, and they have cited resemblances to the compressed, daring style of Metaphysical poets like John Donne who were writing at the beginning of the seventeenth century. Critics have justified the difficulty of the language as a necessary embodiment of the complex and paradoxical qualities

Portions of this chapter are reprinted by permission of the Modern Language Association of America from my article "Shakespeare's Boy Cleopatra, the Decorum of Nature, and the Golden World of Poetry," *PMLA*, Vol. 87 (March, 1972), pp. 201–12 (copyright © 1972 by the Modern Language Association of America).

of the protagonists and their story. But the fact remains that the language is exceedingly difficult.

Another difficulty is Shakespeare's presentation of
Cleopatra; most of the critical debates about *Antony
and Cleopatra* center on the question of her character.
Even those critics who see Antony as the main character cannot ignore the enigma she presents, for
Antony is torn throughout by the conflicting claims
of the Egyptian enchantment Cleopatra embodies and
the Roman honor he can retain only if he gives her
up. After repeated vacillations between Egypt and
Rome, Antony finally chooses Cleopatra and, in fact,
kills himself for love of her; but the dilemma for the
audience remains. If Cleopatra is, as the Romans claim,
a mere "strumpet," then Antony dies "a strumpet's
fool" (I, i). If, however, she is the "peerless" love she
seems to Antony, then his sacrifice is justified and he
dies triumphant. The play provides ample evidence for
both views.

In considering these questions, we ought to remind
ourselves that Shakespeare's Cleopatra was originally
played by a boy. Shortly before her suicide, Cleopatra
tells her women what theatrical treatment awaits them
in Rome if they allow themselves to be taken there for
Caesar's triumph:

> The quick comedians
> Extemporally will stage us, and present
> Our Alexandrian revels; Antony
> Shall be brought drunken forth, and I shall
> see
> Some squeaking Cleopatra boy my greatness
> I' th' posture of a whore.
>
> (V, ii)

Spoken by an actress, these lines are relatively straight-
forward and not greatly significant. They simply tell
us what all admirers of Cleopatra know anyway, this

Paul Hecht as Antony and Salome Jens as Cleopatra in the American Shakespeare Festival Theatre's 1972 production of *Antony and Cleopatra*, directed by Michael Kahn. Most modern productions of the play have stopped short of reviving the practice of the boy actress, and Cleopatra is usually played, as here, by a glamorous woman.

AMERICAN SHAKESPEARE FESTIVAL THEATRE, STRATFORD, CONN.

being the fifth act—that the Romans do not understand her, or Antony, or their love. We need not take the Roman comedians very seriously, for how seriously should we take a performance that misrepresents, of all things, Cleopatra's sex?

But if Shakespeare's Cleopatra is played by a boy, we are likely to notice disturbing similarities between his tragedy and the Roman comedy Cleopatra rejects. Many of Shakespeare's scenes are, in fact, comic;

Antony is "brought drunken forth"; and many of Cleopatra's lines seem better suited to be delivered "in the posture of a whore" than with the dignity of a great queen. She lies to Antony and henpecks him. She hits the messenger and drags him up and down, screaming, "I'll unhair thy head," and "I'll spurn [that is, kick] thine eyes like balls before me" (II, v). When Antony leaves her to go to Rome, she moons like an oversexed schoolgirl:

> O Charmian,
> Where think'st thou he is now? Stands he, or
>   sits he?
> Or does he walk? Or is he on his horse?
> O happy horse, to bear the weight of Antony!
> (I, v)

And, as she reminds us later in the same speech, she is old enough to know better:

> Think on me,
> That am with Phoebus' amorous pinches black,
> And wrinkled deep in time.

In Shakespeare's day the rule of decorum or dramatic propriety, inherited from the ancients and destined to dominate critical theory during the seventeenth and eighteenth centuries, had considerable influence. According to the rule of decorum, each character in a play must display the qualities appropriate to his or her age, sex, and station and no others. Cleopatra refers to this rule when she tells Caesar's envoy:

> If your master
> Would have a queen his beggar, you must tell
>   him
> That majesty, to keep decorum, must
> No less beg than a kingdom.
> (V, ii)

Cleopatra does not "keep decorum"; and under her influence, neither does Antony. Octavius Caesar, the chief representative in the play of Roman values, scornfully describes the way the two lovers violate decorum:

> From Alexandria
> This is the news: he fishes, drinks, and wastes
> The lamps of night in revel; is not more
>   manlike
> Than Cleopatra, nor the queen of Ptolemy
> More womanly than he.
>
> (I, iv)

Forgetting his station as well as his sex, Antony has been willing to "keep the turn of tippling with a slave/... and stand the buffet/With knaves that smell of sweat." This indecorous behavior, according to Caesar, represents a rebellion of Antony's irrational passions against his "judgment": it violates the Roman criterion of rationality as well as the Roman rule of decorum.

There is, then, considerable evidence in Shakespeare's play for taking the Roman comedians seriously; and if Shakespeare's Cleopatra is played by a boy, Shakespeare's treatment of her story seems perilously close to theirs. It is not, however, the same, and even Caesar pays tribute to both lovers' greatness at the end of the play. Although Shakespeare's Cleopatra was played by a boy, and although she does behave badly and even comically in many scenes, she is also the legendary enchantress of the Nile and the subject of the longest and most magnificent panegyric in the play, Enobarbus' great set speech in Act II, scene ii ("The barge she sat in..."). Moreover, Enobarbus is not the only Roman who responds to her charm. Antony gives up one third of the Roman world for her. Dolabella is so impressed by one meeting with her that he betrays Caesar's confidence to give her the information she wants. And most critics, most readers, and most theatergoers have shared their fascination with Cleopatra's glamour and her "infinite variety."

The critical debates about Cleopatra's character, the contradictory evidence within the play, and the ambivalence of our responses to her in the first four acts all stem from an essential ambivalence in the medium in which she is created. For Shakespeare's medium is poetry, but it is also the stage; and the contradictory nature of his Egyptian queen is intimately related to this duality in his art. The evidence against Cleopatra rests mainly on visible spectacles, like her physical assault upon the messenger, or on the events of the plot, like the fact that her pretended suicide sends Antony to his death; and these are the nonverbal aspects of the drama. The evidence for her is mostly in the poetry—the grand hyperbole and the cosmic image that evoke a greatness beyond what has been physically presented. In fact, in *Antony and Cleopatra* Shakespeare seems to be playing these two aspects of his art against each other.

The opening scene exemplifies this duality. We know the Roman position, and the kind of evidence upon which it is based, from the first speech in the play, when Philo tells Demetrius, "This dotage of our general's/O'erflows the measure," and bids him:

> Look, where they come!
> Take but good note, and you shall see in him
> The triple pillar of the world transform'd
> Into a strumpet's fool. Behold and see.

At the end of the scene, Demetrius, having beheld the lovers and taken good note, agrees with Philo's charges; but both Romans have missed the poetry the lovers have spoken and Antony's claim that what he and

Cleopatra have is something that defies measurement and cannot be seen. When Cleopatra asks, "If it be love indeed, tell me how much," Antony replies, "There's beggary in the love that can be reckon'd." When she says, "I'll set a bourn [that is, limit] how far to be belov'd," he responds, "Then must thou needs find out new heaven, new earth." The Romans have missed all this because they have merely "beheld" and "seen" and "reckoned" to determine whether Antony's "dotage o'erflows the measure." At the end of the scene Demetrius remarks only that Antony has refused to hear Caesar's messenger; he asks, "Is Caesar with Antonius priz'd so slight?" To Demetrius, Antony has made an error in measurement. What both Romans miss is that Antony has rejected measurement itself and the whole visible world for a new heaven and new earth that neither we nor Demetrius can see.

Neither do we see the renowned scene on Cleopatra's barge upon the river Cydnus. Instead, we are told about it. Enobarbus—ordinarily a blunt spokesman for a rationalistic and realistic view of the action—is joking with other Romans about Antony's Egyptian life when he suddenly abandons his characteristic ironic prose for poetry. "I will tell you," he says (II, ii), introducing the speech that creates through words alone one of Cleopatra's greatest scenes. Only the telling will do it. The physical spectacle we have been seeing is ambiguous at best. This scene, in contrast, is not physically present. It depends entirely upon poetry, and we shall never see it if we confine ourselves to physical perceptions and rational calculations.

Like Philo's "Behold and see," Enobarbus' "I will tell you" is probably directed to the audience off the stage as well as on it, but this time the audience is invited to abandon physical sight and to contemplate instead a purely poetic and imaginative vision. Shakespeare took most of Enobarbus' speech from the narrative in Sir Thomas North's translation of Plutarch; and the details he added, instead of making the speech more concrete or dramatic, seem to insist that it belongs to another medium. They say, in effect, that the scene by its very nature is impossible to stage, that it can be depicted only in words. Cleopatra's barge, for instance, can perform the miracle of burning on the water because it is "like a burnish'd throne," and "burn'd" is contained in "burnish'd"—not logically, and not visually, but verbally. Such a barge cannot be physically represented but only created, embodied in the alogical shifts that poetry works with words.

Enobarbus' speech is full of hyperbole and paradox —rhetorical indications that its subject cannot be contained within the categories of measurement or logic or physical representation. Enobarbus describes Cleopatra's pavilion as "cloth-of-gold of tissue—/O'er-picturing that Venus where we see/The fancy outwork nature." As a description of yard goods—or of anything else in the visible universe—these lines are notoriously obscure. The lines are quite clear, however, as a description of hyperbole and an indication of the ways it works in this speech. Hyperbole does not describe because it destroys the categories of description; instead, it "o'er-pictures." It does not represent the physical world because it appeals to "the fancy" to "outwork nature" and make us imagine what does not and never can exist in the natural world perceived by physical eyesight and measured by ordinary reckoning. An even better example is the non-description of Cleopatra herself. Enobarbus simply says, "For her own person, it beggar'd all description." He cannot describe Cleopatra's person any more than Antony can measure his love ("There's beggary in the love that can be reckon'd") for both Cleopatra's beauty and Antony's love belong to a universe in which those methods are inadequate—or, to use the language of the play, "beggarly."

In the thoroughly poetic universe of Enobarbus' vision, the ordinary forms of logic are inapplicable, and paradox takes over. The wind from the fans of Cleopatra's attendants "did seem/To glow the delicate cheeks which they did cool,/And what they undid did." Cleopatra can "make defect perfection/And, breathless, power breathe forth."

> Age cannot wither her, nor custom stale
> Her infinite variety. Other women cloy
> The appetites they feed, but she makes hungry
> Where most she satisfies; for vilest things
> Become themselves in her, that the holy priests
> Bless her when she is riggish.

In this final rush of paradoxes, Enobarbus leaps beyond measurement, ordinary morality, and logic itself; for those are the categories our minds design to cope with the world of time and change and limitation, and in the poetic world created by the "fancy" when it "out-works nature," they are no longer necessary or even relevant.

At this point Enobarbus' creation is complete, but it is severely limited. For one thing, it is purely verbal, and for another, it is based on illusion. Here, as in Plutarch, Cleopatra's splendor is a *tour de force* of artifice. The aging queen, who earlier described herself as "black" with the "amorous pinches" of the sun and "wrinkled deep in time" (I, v), has staged an elaborate spectacle, complete with stage props, background music, minor actors, and a carefully constructed setting. And, as Enobarbus five times reminds us, the whole thing belongs to the world of seeming. Cleopatra's barge is "*like* a burnish'd throne." The "pretty dimpled boys" who wield her fans are *"like* smiling Cupids." The wind they make "did *seem* to glow the delicate cheeks" they cooled. The gentlewomen tending her are *"like* the Nereides." The barge is steered by "a *seeming* mermaid" (italics all mine). In creating these wonders, Cleopatra deals in likenesses and seemings, not in the stuff the Romans—or the Roman in all of us—would call reality.

Likenesses and seemings are in fact Cleopatra's stock in trade throughout the play. Her bewildering parade of shifting moods, motives, and strategems has led most critics to conclude that her one salient quality is, paradoxically, her lack of one—the magnificent inconstancy which Enobarbus calls "infinite variety" and which her enemies condemn as treachery. And yet, behind all her turnings, one motive remains constant: she is a dedicated contriver and performer of shows—so much so that we are never sure how to take her.

In the opening scene Cleopatra makes a brief statement that seems to sound the keynote of her character: "I'll seem the fool I am not." Seeming is Cleopatra's great defect, but it is also her consummate virtue. She seems worse than a fool when she sends Antony a false report of her suicide that moves him to take his own life; but although she unwittingly causes his death with this ruse, she consciously provides for his triumph over Octavius Caesar with another. At the end of the play (V, ii) Cleopatra makes great Caesar seem an "ass unpolicied" when she uses her deceptive arts to thwart his plans to lead her in triumph in Rome. And even though Antony is already dead, Cleopatra imagines she hears him "mock the luck of Caesar" as she prepares for her splendid suicide—the "noble act" that will defeat Caesar and reunite the triumphant lovers.

In the first four acts Cleopatra is a thoroughly ambivalent figure, and her ambivalence is directly connected to the ambivalence of Shakespeare's theatrical strategy. Insofar as we respond to the poetry, we want to accept Cleopatra's claim that what she does on stage belongs only to the world of seeming and that the truth about her is the greatness we never see. But insofar as we behold and see and measure and evaluate her actions, we are forced, like Enobarbus, to regard the show of magnificence as the seeming—all the more so, in fact, since, unlike Enobarbus, we have not yet seen it.

The conflict between the poetic Cleopatra and the theatrical one—between the greatness evoked by Shakespeare's words and the foolishness enacted on his stage—culminates in the "boy my greatness" speech (V, ii). When Cleopatra says the Roman comedians would have "some squeaking Cleopatra boy my great-ness/I' th' posture of a whore," she directly opposes her claim to greatness against the evidence of the Roman theater. But if Shakespeare's Cleopatra is, in fact, a boy, then the Roman theater she describes is Shakespeare's too; and there is suddenly a new element in the conflict. We know now that everything—what we have beheld and seen no less than what we have heard and imagined—is simply show. The Egyptian queen contracts for a moment to the squeaking boy who acts her part, and for that moment the entire fabric of dramatic illusion is torn. The "boy my great-ness" speech has, in effect, destroyed the reality prin-ciple within the play, and all we are left with is theater.

The speech thus prepares us to reorganize our disparate and jarring impressions of Cleopatra into a new synthesis. Cleopatra can now redefine herself in a new show—the spectacular suicide by which she will finally show us what Enobarbus saw upon the river Cydnus. Enobarbus' vision of magnificence is a purely poetic vision, staged before the mind's eye on an empty stage. In Cleopatra's suicide scene, however, the vision is evoked by all the resources of Shakespeare's theater. The stage, no less than the audience, is now freed from the demands of realism and rational plausibility, and for once we can see on it what drew Antony from Rome and turned Enobarbus into a poet.

That Cleopatra's suicide is a show would be apparent in the theater, for even the costume change with which she prepares for it takes place on stage: "Show me, my women, like a queen," she says. "Go fetch/My best attires; I am again for Cydnus/To meet Mark Antony" (V, ii). Cleopatra commands her women to "show" her "like a queen"; but for the characters on stage, and for the audience as well, the likeness becomes reality. After Cleopatra's death, Charmian says, "golden Phoebus never be beheld/Of eyes again so royal!" The suicide, she says, "is well done, and fitting for a princess/Descended of so many royal kings." Caesar, discovering Cleopatra dead, says, "Bravest at the last,/She levell'd at our purposes, and, being royal,/Took her own way." The word "royal" echoes through the scene like a refrain, but at this point in the play we have more than words to convince us. When Cleopatra puts on her robe and crown here, they serve to define in a fully theatrical way the nature of a queen who is so thoroughly involved with the world of art and illusion that she is incomprehensible except within its own terms. Cleopatra is wearing the robes and crown of a queen. She is acting like a queen —committing suicide with grand poetry on her lips. And for an audience in a theater, the costume they see, the poetry they hear, and the act they see performed are sufficient; for they satisfy the only kind of criteria for truth that are available within the context of the theater.

After she calls for her royal costume, Cleopatra proceeds to answer one by one all the charges brought

against her by the Romans and made credible to the
audience by her actions in the earlier parts of the
play. If the Romans called her Antony's "strumpet,"
she now calls him her "husband." She drank him under
the table, but now she renounces forever the "juice of
Egypt's grape." She was a "boggler ever," but now,
she says, "My resolution's plac'd . . . /I am marble-
constant." We can accept this redefinition of her
character without reservation because Cleopatra has
already made the ultimate reservation for us. We know
that the whole thing is a show—the physical spectacle
no less than the language—and knowing that, we are
free to meet it on its own terms. We have entered a
fully theatrical world where a boy Cleopatra can put
on her royalty with its emblems. The Roman objections to Cleopatra are no longer valid because they
depend upon our faith in the factuality of the things
we have beheld and seen in the earlier parts of the
play. And the boy Cleopatra has destroyed that faith
by reminding us of the ultimate fact that everything
we have seen is theater.

At this point, we might associate the Roman view of
Cleopatra with the kind of perceptions we have in the
real world or a realistic theater, and the Egyptian
view, evoked in Enobarbus' poetry and finally shown
in Cleopatra's monument, with the kind of experience
we have in a poetic theater. In the Roman theater, the
boy Cleopatra would appear as he was in fact in
Shakespeare's London, a squeaking boy. In Egypt, and
to the Egyptian imagination, he would be the queen
he enacted on Shakespeare's stage. This same kind of
association holds true for other Shakespeare boy-
heroines. For instance, in *The Merchant of Venice*
Portia is disguised as a boy in Venice but appears in
Belmont as the girl she truly is. Like Rome, Venice
is a realistic world, concerned with the things that can
be beheld and seen and reckoned; and like Egypt,

Belmont is a world of love and music and fantastic occurrences. In both plays, the realistic world sees the heroine disguised as the boy she actually was in Shakespeare's London, while the imaginative world shows her true femininity—a truth that is paradoxically identical with the illusion presented on Shakespeare's stage.

Traditional Shakespearean criticism tends to dismiss the boy actress as a quaint limitation in the Elizabethan theater, which Shakespeare, being a great artist, somehow managed to disguise; and even the modern vogue for Elizabethan-style Shakespeare production has usually (but not always) stopped short of reviving the boy actress. Still, there is a dimension of Cleopatra's greatness—and of her maker's—so intensely theatrical that it can only be "boyed." Like his devious, resourceful Egyptian queen, Shakespeare could "make defect perfection."

Coriolanus

Like *Julius Caesar* and *Antony and Cleo-patra*, *Coriolanus* is closely based upon one of Plutarch's *Lives*, and the three plays are often studied together as a distinct group, the "Roman plays." Since *Coriolanus* is close to *Julius Caesar* in its methods and concerns, the two plays serve in a number of ways to illuminate each other. In both, the subject and theme are overwhelmingly political and ideological. In both, the protagonist is a rather cold and distant figure: Coriolanus, in fact, seems positively forbidding.[13] In both, the mob is a major character. Like Brutus, Coriolanus faces several antagonists during the course of the play but finds his real nemesis in his inability to deal with the lower orders in the state or their analogues in his own psyche.

Shakespeare seems in both these Roman plays, set in remote, pre-Christian times, to be exploring various forms of bad government. Brutus' fatal flaw is his inordinate faith in the common people; he fails to recognize that they, like the lower elements in the individual soul, require government from above for their own good and for the good of the commonwealth. Coriolanus sees clearly that the lower orders are incapable

of reason and self-determination, but, blinded by in-
ordinate contempt for the common people, he fails to
recognize that the higher orders are bound to the lower
by obligations of love and duty as well as prerogatives
of rule. While Brutus loves the plebeians too much,
Coriolanus loves them too little; and his failure, even
more than Brutus', illustrates the fatal effects of pride
in public life.

Underlying *Julius Caesar* as an implicit norm defining the fallacy in Brutus' thinking is the familiar
Elizabethan analogy between the body natural and
the body politic. A version of the analogy is explicitly stated in the opening scene of *Coriolanus,* and
it establishes the ideological context for the subsequent
action. *Coriolanus* begins, as *Julius Caesar* does, when a
company of citizens bursts upon the stage, but here
they are already an undifferentiated mob, armed with
staves and clubs and bent on mutiny. Hungry, they
are determined to rise against the patricians who have
deprived them, but Menenius answers their complaints
with the fable of the belly: "There was a time when
all the body's members/Rebell'd against the belly,"
accusing it of remaining "idle and unactive," "like a
gulf . . . /I' th' midst o' th' body," hoarding food but
never sharing the labor of the other parts. The belly
answers their complaints by arguing that although he
does "receive the general food at first," he serves as
the store-house and the shop/Of the whole body,"
distributing the nourishing flour to all the parts but
retaining only the bran for himself. Menenius draws
the moral: "The senators of Rome are this good belly,/
And you the mutinous members. . . . / . . . you shall
find/No public benefit which you receive/But it proceeds or comes from them to you/And no way from
yourselves" (I, i).

The commons are "almost thoroughly persuaded"
by Menenius' arguments; for, he says, although

"abundantly they lack discretion,/Yet are they pass-
ing cowardly," and he has also reminded them that the
senate will defend its prerogatives with force (I, i).
And yet, the citizens have displayed considerable discretion during the course of this scene. When they
first enter, they declare their special hatred for Caius
Marcius, and all their charges against him are verified
by his subsequent behavior. They know he hates them,
and, more important, they recognize that his military
services to Rome are motivated by personal pride and
a desire to please his mother rather than by patriotism.
Moreover, the second citizen interrupts Menenius'
fable of the belly with a list of objections that shows
his own understanding of the analogy is equal—and
perhaps superior—to Menenius'. To the second citizen,
the belly is "the sink o' th' body" and should not
restrain "The kingly-crowned head, the vigilant eye,/
The counsellor heart, the arm our soldier,/Our steed
the leg, the tongue our trumpeter." To the sensual
Menenius, who "loves a cup of hot wine with not a
drop of allaying Tiber in't" (II, i), the belly represents
the Roman senators; in his analogy their rights and
duties begin and end with the accumulation and distri-
bution of the means of sustenance. But the second
citizen's analogy emphasizes not the belly but the
head—the emblem of the authority tragically lacking
in the Rome of *Coriolanus*.

Coriolanus, according to the analogy, is the arm of
the body politic, the soldier who defends it but who
should be subject in an ideal state to the rational control of the king (the head) and to the good advice of
the counsellors (the heart). But Rome has no king,
and when Coriolanus defeats the Volsces, he seems
the natural choice for consul. His tragedy, and that of
his country, stems from his utter incapacity for rule
and from the lack of any better candidate to whom he
can give his allegiance.

As a soldier, Coriolanus knows no other authority than force, but force alone is not sufficient to govern a nation, for it is the authority that one enemy exercises over another, and Coriolanus ends, as he must, by making his countrymen his enemies. Even in the opening scene Coriolanus would put down the rebellion as if the mutinous citizens were enemies to be destroyed rather than misguided members of the same body as himself:

> Would the nobility lay aside their ruth
> And let me use my sword, I'd make a quarry
> With thousands of these quarter'd slaves as
>   high
> As I could pick my lance.

The demagogue Junius Brutus, who speaks as one of the "tongues o' th' common mouth," is undoubtedly right when he charges, "You speak o' th' people/As if you were a god to punish, not/A man of their infirmity" (III, i), for Coriolanus's inability to love the people is directly related to his enormous personal pride.

That same terrible pride also makes it impossible for Coriolanus to subject his passionate will to the rule of reason. In Renaissance theory, the good ruler, the "kingly crowned head," was the political embodiment of reason, but Coriolanus is finally as irrational as the mob that destroys him. All his enemies, from the peoples' tribunes in Act III to Aufidius at the end, have only to offend his pride in public to evoke the irrational rage in Coriolanus that will, in turn, evoke the irrational fury of the mob. Coriolanus cannot control the mob because he cannot control his own passions. Their automatic, mindless rage is the exact analogue to his, and the two collaborate to destroy him.

In Act III, scene ii of *Coriolanus* Volumnia (Fay Compton, at right) and Menenius (William Squire, center) persuade Coriolanus (Richard Burton, second from right) to speak mildly to the enraged citizens who have gathered in the marketplace. This production of *Coriolanus* was directed by Michael Benthall during the Old Vic's 1953–54 London season.

ANGUS MCBEAN PHOTOGRAPH, HARVARD THEATRE COLLECTION

The only character in the play who can rule Coriolanus is his mother. In Act III it is Volumnia who persuades him to beg the plebeians' pardon in the Forum, even though she knows as well as he does that he will have to suppress and belie his true feelings to do so. The results, of course, are disastrous: Coriolanus has hardly begun to speak when the tribunes goad him into a furious outburst that provokes the people to banish him. In Act V Volumnia again persuades Coriolanus to a disastrous act when she prevails upon him to spare Rome from invasion by his Volscian army. Even as he prepares to obey her, Coriolanus foresees the cost of his obedience:

> O, my mother, mother! O!
> You have won a happy victory to Rome;
> But, for your son,—believe it, O believe it—,
> Most dangerously you have with him prevail'd,
> If not most mortal to him.
>
> (V, iii)

When Coriolanus returns to Corioli, his old enemy Aufidius uses Coriolanus' decision to spare Rome as a pretext to have him murdered.

Plutarch describes Coriolanus as an exemplar of the special virtue of his time and place:

> Now in those days valiantness was honoured in Rome above all other virtues; which they call *virtus*, by the name of virtue itself, as including in that general name all other special virtues besides. So that *virtus* in the Latin was as much as valiantness.[14]

That special virtue, *virtus*, might also be described as "manliness," for its root is *vir*, the Latin word for "man."[15] And Coriolanus' entire career seems, in a way, to represent a long pursuit of his own manliness.

In Shakespeare as in Plutarch, Coriolanus is depicted as his mother's son, the product of her education, but Volumnia is a thoroughly manly woman, almost a caricature of the stern virtues of a Roman matron and an ardent devotee of the ideal of *virtus*. She tells Virgilia, "I sprang not more in joy at first hearing he was a man-child than now in first seeing he had proved himself a man [that is, by valor in battle]" (I, iii). When Virgilia expresses horror at the thought of her husband as Volumnia delightedly pictures him, "with bloody brow," Volumnia instructs her in the ideal of *virtus*—a bloody brow "more becomes a man/Than gilt his trophy [that is, monument]"—and in its peculiar aesthetic:

> The breasts of Hecuba,
> When she did suckle Hector, look'd not lovelier
> Than Hector's forehead when it spit forth blood
> At Grecian sword, contemning.

Volumnia continues to rebuke her daughter-in-law for every expression of feminine softness or scruples, making it clear that the education she gave her son was anything but effeminate. Ironically, however, it suffered from the opposite deficiency: Volumnia has taught Coriolanus his morbid horror of everything associated with femininity, the virtues no less than the vices, and his exaggerated devotion to a limited ideal of manliness.

In Act III Coriolanus is afraid to apologize to the people lest he lose his manhood and take on "some harlot's spirit" or his "throat of war be turn'd/ . . . into a pipe small as an eunuch's, or the virgin voice/That babies lull asleep" and "schoolboys' tears take up/The glasses of [his] sight" (III, ii). Coriolanus cannot tolerate any threat to his masculinity, and when Aufidius calls him a "boy of tears" in Act V, he responds with furious denials of the unbearable epithet:

> Measureless liar, thou hast made my heart,
> Too great for what contains it. "Boy!" O slave!
> . . . .
> Cut me to pieces, Volsces; men and lads,

> Stain all your edges on me. "Boy!" False
>   hound!
> If you have writ your annals true, 'tis there
> That, like an eagle in a dove-cote, I
> Flutter'd your Volscians in Corioli;
> Alone I did it. "Boy!"
>
> (V, vi)

Desperate to prove to the assembled Volsces that he is not a boy, Coriolanus presents the only evidence of manhood that he knows—the military valor by which he beat those same Volsces in the past. The mob calls, predictably, for his death, and Coriolanus dies as he lived in an extravagant, self-destructive attempt to prove his manhood.

In *Coriolanus*, as in none of his other tragedies, Shakespeare gives us a great deal of information about the hero's childhood and education; and we are repeatedly told that he is the product of his mother's teaching. Like his mother and his compatriots, Coriolanus conceives the manly ideal as embodied in the soldier, the fighting arm of the state; but in Renaissance theory the father in a family, like the king in a state, served the function of the head—the embodiment of the governing principle of reason. Coriolanus' Rome is a defective state, for it has no king; his family has no father; and he himself has no capacity for rational control of his passions. In Act III, trying to convince Coriolanus to apologize to the plebeians, Volumnia says, "I have a heart as little apt as yours./But yet a brain that leads my use of anger/To better vantage" (III, ii). Coriolanus cannot follow her good advice, not only because he lacks her controlling brain but also because he shares her unloving heart. In her single-minded devotion to the masculine ideal of *virtus* ("Thy valiantness was mine," she says in III, ii, "thou suck'st it from me") Volumnia has deprived her son of the feminine virtues he also needs. Volumnia has a man's valor, but she lacks a woman's compassion. Like Coriolanus, Volumnia despises the common people, just as she despises her daughter-in-law's feminine virtues.

What Coriolanus has learned from his stern, Roman mother is to despise the maternal virtues that sustain life and bind the human community together. And yet, at least at one point, Volumnia seems to recognize that her son's need to assert his manhood is morbid and self-defeating. Arguing that an apology to the plebeians would be a betrayal of his manhood, Coriolanus asks his mother, "Would you have me/False to my nature? Rather say I play/The man I am" (III, ii). She responds prophetically, "You might have been enough the man you are,/With striving less to be so."

Marcius' greatest prodigy of *virtus* (commemorated in his surname, Coriolanus), his solitary battle within the gates of Corioli, demonstrates his extraordinary valor but also signifies his essential isolation. When his own soldiers try to retreat from battle he threatens them to fight "or, by the fires of heaven, I'll leave the foe/And make my wars on you" (I, iv). When the tribune Sicinius calls Coriolanus a traitor, Coriolanus is goaded to ungovernable rage, just as he will be when Aufidius calls him a boy, and for the same reasons: in both cases the epithet expresses a truth Coriolanus cannot bear to hear. Just as his extraordinary valor is a desperate effort to prove a manhood he never fully attains, his extraordinary military services are done in the name of a country he never really loves. Coriolanus answers Sicinius' charge with a reckless fury that incites the Roman people to banish him; and, ironically, as soon as they do, he becomes literally a traitor, going over to the enemy and marching with the Volscians against Rome. As the plebeians recognize from the first, Coriolanus is no more capable of loving his country than he is of loving them, for the ideal of *virtus* that animates him does not include love or loyalty to anything other than itself.

Although we get a great deal of information about Coriolanus' character and motivations, he remains from first to last a curiously distant figure. Most of what we know about him comes from the comments of other characters, many of them scornful or condescending; and even though we learn about the education that made him what he is, we never see him change or grow or learn from his experience. His characterization is curiously objective, more like an anatomy of a static figure than a dramatic portrayal of a complicated, changing human personality. His tragedy is not so much a revelation of a universal human predicament as an illustration of the inadequacy of the Roman ideal of *virtus*.

In *Antony and Cleopatra* the opposition between Octavius' Rome and Cleopatra's Egypt is characterized as an opposition between a purely masculine world and a purely feminine one, between the masculine pleasures of military conquest and political power and the feminine ones of love and imagination and soft luxury. The Romans in that play abhor Cleopatra's feminine vices, and one of their chief objections to Antony's Egyptian life is that it has made him effeminate. At the end both lovers transcend the limitations of their worlds to become, in a sense, androgynous, to find their full humanity in triumphant union with each other. In the Rome of Coriolanus the characters, like their society, remain fragmented.

When Volumnia first comes to plead with her son to spare Rome, Coriolanus vows, "I'll never/Be such a gosling to obey instinct, but stand/As if a man were author of himself/And knew no other kin" (V, iii), expressing at once his pride, his isolation, his repudiation of his place in nature, and his denial of his own humanity. Nevertheless, even then the mute femininity of Virgilia's "doves' eyes" moves him to pity and softens his pride ("I melt, and am not/Of stronger earth than others"); and at the end of the scene, when he succumbs to the women's pleas, he seems to discover, at last, his own humanity and to accept the feminine side of his nature. He admits that he is crying and that his decision to spare the city is prompted by feminine feeling within himself ("Not of a woman's tenderness to be/Requires nor child nor woman's face to see./I have sat too long"). The world Coriolanus lives in, however, assigns no value to femininity or feminine emotions. Aufidius says contemptuously, "At a few drops of women's rheum, which are/As cheap as lies, he sold the blood and labour/Of our great action" (V, vi); and when he taunts Coriolanus as a "boy of tears," Coriolanus succumbs once more to the destructive ideal of *virtus* and dies asserting his manhood.

Coriolanus is a much less attractive character than the Brutus of *Julius Caesar*, and his fall results much more obviously from his own shortcomings; but the Rome in which he lives is also a worse place than Brutus' Rome, and Coriolanus, like Brutus, is both victim and exemplar of the defects of his world. The vulgar mob in *Coriolanus*, like the one in *Julius Caesar*, is a dangerous beast, subject to no lawful king, incapable of governing itself, and therefore easy prey to any demagogue who knows how to manipulate it. Coriolanus is a heroic warrior, but he cannot govern his own temper or the furious mobs who are its external counterparts, for he has nothing to lead him but the mindless and heartless principle of *virtus*. Like *Julius Caesar*, *Coriolanus* lacks the emotional appeal and the moral complexity of Shakespeare's greatest tragedies, but it continues his exploration of the interconnection between the structure of the state and the disposition of the individual human soul. The Roman state in

these plays may not become, as does Hamlet's Denmark
or Lear's England or Macbeth's Scotland, a microcosm
of the universe and a stage for deeds whose consequences reach from heaven to hell; but it does serve
as a macrocosm of the human psyche, and its troubles
hold up a mirror to our own sins and sufferings. The
Rome in these plays is a purely political entity, a state
without a king struggling to govern itself. And the
heroes are men who struggle with their own problems
without the aid of heavenly grace or wholeness of
being.

Timon of Athens

Timon of Athens has been described as a failure, as Shakespeare's greatest tragedy, as a great play which is not a tragedy but a satire, and as an incomplete version of a potentially great tragedy. The last description is probably the best. There is no record that Timon of Athens was ever played or printed during Shakespeare's lifetime, and the date of its composition is unknown. The only text we have, from the First Folio of 1623, contains so many defects and anomalies that most scholars believe the play was never finished. Some of the older critics conjectured that it was Shakespeare's adaptation of a lost play or another writer's revision of Shakespeare's play, but the prevailing opinion today is that the entire text is Shakespeare's, although the extent and seriousness of its imperfections are still debated.

The story of Timon, based primarily upon an account in Plutarch's Life of Antony, bears enough resemblances to Antony's story, and to Lear's as well, to make this play an interesting subject for students of Shakespeare. Like Antony, Timon has a magnanimous spirit, a thirst for infinity that expresses itself in sensual excess and extravagant generosity. Here as in Antony *and Cleopatra* food and appetite are dominant images that evoke a life of boundless indulgence and soft luxury; and in both plays the hero's enemies are cold, calculating politicians. Like Lear, Timon is a victim of ingratitude, for he dissipates his great fortune in gifts to false friends and suitors who turn against him when he is destitute. Like Lear, he gives "all" and receives "nothing" in return, and his expressions of defiance and misanthropy rival Lear's in furious eloquence.

Despite these similarities, however, Timon's sufferings lack the emotional impact and philosophical significance that engage the audience in the tragedies of Antony and Lear. Timon's pessimism is even deeper than Lear's, but the audience does not necessarily share it; it seems a personal response to a personal disaster and not, as Lear's does, a description of a metaphysical cataclysm that threatens the audience as well as the actors on stage. Timon's conversion from optimistic philanthropy to pessimistic misanthropy is more absolute than Antony's vacillations between Egypt and Rome, but it does not engage the audience in the profound ethical and epistemological conflicts that make Antony's dilemma theirs as well. Timon simply moves from one excess to another, and although he evokes the audience's sympathy, he does not become their surrogate. Timon's tragedy thus seems curiously private and personal, never fully involving the audience, or even the other characters in the play.

To be sure, the Athenian state is conquered at the end, and Timon's enemies will be punished, but these are Alcibiades' doings and not Timon's, and the connection between the two protagonists seems tenuous and contrived. Timon gives Alcibiades the gold to pay his soldiers, and his refusal to lead the Athenian army insures Alcibiades' victory; but the victory still belongs to Albiciades and not to Timon, and Alcibiades is motivated by the Athenians' ingratitude to him, not by their ingratitude to Timon. As a result, the problems raised by the play are not really settled by the ending. Timon dies in despair and misanthropy, and Alcibiades' promise to establish good order in Athens fails to make Timon's sufferings meaningful, for there is no indication that Timon's ruin was necessary to achieve it.

Alcibiades' character, like the relationship between him and Timon, seems incomplete and inconsistent. With further development, these inconsistencies might have indicated stages in the evolution of his character and the progress of his action. But as the play stands, there are not enough connecting links to indicate how or why the changes occur.

In Act III, scene v, Alcibiades petitions the Athenian senate to pardon a soldier friend of his who has rashly killed another man in anger. The senators refuse, arguing that the truly valiant man can suffer wrongs stoically rather than give in to anger, but their argument is badly undercut by their actions when Alcibiades' repeated pleadings provoke their own anger and they banish him. Their ingratitude to Alcibiades for his military service to Athens parallels the Athenians' ingratitude to Timon and contrasts with Alcibiades' loyalty to his condemned friend. But Alcibiades' own position is not unassailable: his trade is warfare, and all his arguments rest upon the assumption that war is good. His friend has fought valiantly for Athens and should be pardoned; the crime was a deed of "valour," done "with a noble fury and fair spirit"; the senate owes Alcibiades a favor in return for his own military services; and, finally, "law is strict, and war is nothing more."

When Timon greets Alcibiades in Act IV, he echoes Alcibiades' equation of war and law but uses it to condemn the law, not to justify war:

> Follow thy drum;
> With man's blood paint the ground, gules,
>   gules [red (heraldic term)].
> Religious canons, civil laws are cruel;
> Then what should war be?
>
> (IV, iii)

He encourages Alcibiades to destroy Athens in terms that vividly evoke the barbarity of warfare. "Let not thy sword skip one," he says:

> Let not the virgin's cheek
> Make soft thy trenchant sword; for those
>   milk-paps,
> That through the window bars bore at men's
>   eyes,
> Are not within the leaf of pity writ,
> But set them down horrible traitors. Spare not
>   the babe,
> Whose dimpled smiles from fools exhaust
>   their mercy;
> Think it a bastard, whom the oracle
> Hath doubtfully pronounc'd thy throat shall
>   cut,
> And mince it sans remorse. Swear against
>   objects;
> Put armour on thine ears and on thine eyes;
> Whose proof nor yells of mothers, maids, nor
>   babes,
> Nor sight of priests in holy vestments bleeding,
> Shall pierce a jot. There's gold to pay thy
>   soldiers,
> Make large confusion; and, thy fury spent,
> Confounded be thyself!
>
> (IV, iii)

Alcibiades does not "make large confusion": at the end of the play he decides to spare the city and introduce a rule of justice and order, but his last-minute

announcement that he will do so is probably as much
a surprise to the audience as it is to the Athenians,
and his motivation remains obscure. Perhaps the audience is meant to assume that Alcibiades has changed as
a result of his contact with Timon, but the why and
how and when of the change are open to conjecture;
and without answers to these questions, the meaning
of Alcibiades' story—and its relationship to Timon's
—is not clear.

Two whores accompany Alcibiades when he meets
Timon in the woods in Act IV, and when he leaves
the stage, they go with him. The next time Alcibiades
appears, however, at the beginning of the last scene in
the play, his opening words are, "Sound to this coward
and lascivious town/Our terrible approach," and he
goes on to condemn the Athenians for indulgence in
"licentious" pleasures. His own licentiousness, like his
fury, has apparently been purged, but the process by
which it happened is neither enacted on the stage nor
reported, another troublesome omission that tends to
obscure the nature and significance of Alcibiades'
action.

These and other structural weaknesses have pre-
vented *Timon of Athens* from sharing the theatrical
success of Shakespeare's other tragedies. However, the
richness of its language and imagery and the pro-
fundity of its themes remain impressive, and a few
critics, concentrating on those aspects of the drama,
have ranked it with the greatest of Shakespeare's plays.
Richly evocative images of gold, of food, and of
nature are interwoven with each other and with the
major themes of the play to suggest a profound significance in Timon's story.

At the end of the play, Alcibiades suggests that the
very excess of Timon's grief and pessimism achieved
a kind of nobility that set him above nature and redeemed his faults:

> Though thou abhorr'dst in us our human
>   griefs,
> Scorn'dst our brain's flow and those our drop-
>   lets which
> From niggard nature fall, yet rich conceit
> Taught thee to make vast Neptune weep for
>   aye
> On thy low grave, on faults forgiven.
>
> (V, iv)

The spectacular opulence of Act I, Timon's eloquent poetry, and the richly symbolic verbal texture of the play tend to support Alcibiades' suggestion, but the play still seems incomplete. Alcibiades' final tribute to Timon is very brief; and, like the play it concludes, it suggests a nobility and a tragic significance that it does not quite manage to define.

SHAKESPEARE'S TRAGEDIES ON STAGE

Shakespeare wrote his plays to be acted on stage. The first edition of his collected plays was not published until seven years after his death, and although about half of the plays were first published during his lifetime, there is no evidence that he saw any of them through the press.

Until 1608 Shakespeare's company performed in an outdoor, public theater. Its exact structure is not known, but contemporary accounts of other public theaters, together with evidence in the dialogue and stage directions in the plays, provide a fairly good idea of its main features. The stage was a raised platform, which extended out into a yard or pit where members of the audience stood. The pit was surrounded by raised galleries where other spectators sat. Since the galleries were arranged in vertical tiers and the stage protruded a good way into the pit, none of the spectators, even those seated in the galleries, was very far from an actor standing at the edge of the stage. Part of the stage, as well as the pit, was unroofed, and the plays were performed in the daytime.

Two barriers that make Shakespeare's asides and

soliloquies awkward in a modern proscenium theater—
the actual distance between audience and stage and the
psychological distance between a lit stage and a darkened auditorium—thus did not exist in Shakespeare's
theater. Instead of throwing his words hundreds of feet
into a darkened theater, an actor could actually stand
much closer to members of the audience than to other
actors on stage who were not supposed to hear him.[1]

There was, naturally, no curtain at the front of this
stage, and no elaborate scenery to set up or remove.
As a result, scenes on the Elizabethan stage were
closely juxtaposed, allowing for symbolic effects when
abrupt shifts from one scene to another made implicit
comments on the action. Moreover, setting in a Shakespeare play tends to be symbolic rather than literal.
When the location of a scene is important, one of the
characters will let us know what it is. When no location is specified, no specific location is to be imagined.
In *Antony and Cleopatra*, for example, the scenes range
from Egypt to Rome to Syria—to virtually every part
of the known world—but Rome and Egypt are not
so much geographical states as states of mind.

Elizabethan theatrical records show that the companies took pains to dress the actors in splendid
costumes, but the costumes were designed for symbolic and spectacular effects and not for literal historical accuracy. A contemporary sketch of a scene from
Titus Andronicus shows a curious mixture of Roman
and Elizabethan costume; in *Julius Caesar*, an anach-
ronistic clock strikes, and the conspirators wear hats.

Shakespeare's plays were written for a very verbal
theater. To raise the sun at the end of the dark opening scene in *Hamlet*, Shakespeare has Horatio say:

> But, look, the morn, in russet mantle clad,
> Walks o'er the dew of yon high eastern hill.

To evoke the night of Banquo's murder, he has Macbeth tell us:

> Light thickens, and the crow
> Makes wing to th' rooky wood:
> Good things of day begin to droop and
> drowse,
> Whiles night's black agents to their preys do
> rouse.
>
> (III, ii)

And no stage lighting or cinematic effects can reproduce the moonlit night in Capulet's garden that Shakespeare's words created for an Elizabethan audience in their daylit theater.

Hamlet tells the actors who come to Elsinore that the purpose of their art is "to hold, as 'twere, the mirror up to nature" (III, ii); his words tell us less about Elizabethan acting technique (which was probably more declamatory than naturalistic) than they do about the way Shakespeare's plays involved their audiences. Shakespeare's theater was called the Globe, the loft above the stage was called the "heavens," and the region beneath it was known as "hell." Shakespeare's stage represented the entire world, but it was not so much a picture as a microcosm of the life it represented. In later, proscenium theaters the audience would peer into a picture frame to spy on the characters' imaginary lives, but in Shakespeare's theater the stage was surrounded by a daylit audience whose members could see and respond to each other as well as the actors on stage; instead of looking through a window to spy on other people's lives, they looked into a mirror that showed them their own.

In the prologue to *Henry V* Shakespeare admits the limitations of his stage:

> Can this cockpit hold
> The vasty fields of France? Or may we cram
> Within this wooden O the very casques
> That did affright the air at Agincourt?

But he also celebrates its limitless resources:

> a crooked figure may
> Attest in little place a million;
> And let us, ciphers to this great accompt,
> On your imaginary forces work.

"Piece out our imperfections with your thoughts," he says, "and make imaginary puissance." The imaginative force of Shakespeare's words made his audience his collaborators. Sitting or standing close to the stage, and sometimes even upon it, they were not so much spectators as participants in the events enacted there.

In 1642 the Puritan regime prohibited public theatrical performances, and when the theaters were reopened after the Restoration of King Charles II eighteen years later, the movement toward more spectacular methods of presentation, which had already begun before the Interregnum, proceeded rapidly. Movable painted scenery, elaborate stage effects and costumes, the use of actresses instead of boy actors for women's parts—all these innovations tended to emphasize the visual aspects of the drama and diminish the importance of the verbal and symbolic aspects. Furthermore, the introduction of the proscenium arch and the gradual retreat of most of the stage from the apron in front of the proscenium arch to the framed box behind it tended to separate the audiences in these large theaters from the actors and to transform theatergoing from an experience in which the audience could actively participate to something much more like a spectator sport.

After the Restoration, William Davenant was given

control of a theatrical company and the rights to perform a number of Shakespeare's plays. He had staged royal masques before the closing of the theaters, and he now proceeded to devise spectacular visual effects for the public theater. His versions of Shakespeare's plays set the new style—with elaborate scenery and theatrical machines, flying witches, gorgeous tableaux, and other *tours de force*.

Davenant's taste for elaborate spectacle and his textual revisions of the plays he produced foreshadowed the shape Shakespearean production would take throughout the late-seventeenth and eighteenth centuries. Like his contemporaries and successors, Davenant followed the neoclassic dramatic ideals of decorum, verisimilitude, and poetic justice. Obscurities, ambiguities, and improprieties were purged from Shakespeare's language; minor characters who had no obvious plot function were removed from the plays, as were comic scenes in the tragedies. Love interest and moral instruction were added to better serve the neoclassical notion of the purpose of literary art—to delight and teach. Nahum Tate's version of *King Lear*, which supplanted Shakespeare's on the English stage for over a hundred years, shows the sort of "improvements" that were introduced to suit the taste of the new age. Tate removed the Fool, simplified the language, and added a love story involving Edgar and Cordelia to explain Cordelia's behavior in the opening scene and, even more important, to provide a poetically just and happy ending in the marriage of the virtuous lovers.

Great actors like Thomas Betterton (1635–1710), David Garrick (1717–1779), and John Philip Kemble (1757–1823) and actresses like Sarah Siddons (1755–1831) dominated the stage from the Restoration through the early nineteenth century and influenced the style of Shakespearean productions. Betterton succeeded Davenant as manager of the Duke's Company, and although he continued Davenant's practice of improving the plays with elaborate spectacular effects, the poetic and emotional power of his acting, especially in roles like Hamlet, Macbeth, and Othello, won extravagant praise. In the early years of the eighteenth century, after Betterton's death, Shakespearean acting declined, affected by neoclassic demands for dignity and decorum; but in the 1740s David Garrick emerged to replace stilted declamations with a stunning new realism. Although Garrick was not above altering the plays (for instance, he completely revised the ending of *Hamlet*), he also restored much that had been cut by his predecessors.

The dominant figure during the early years of the nineteenth century, John Philip Kemble, reverted to the older style of acting, dignified and formal. The greatly enlarged theaters of the period (the rebuilt Covent Garden held about three thousand people and Drury Lane even more) undoubtedly had something to do with Kemble's preference for the grand gesture and the slow declamation, but the neoclassic bent of his own taste might have required them anyway. Kemble preferred Tate's *King Lear* to the more Shakespearean version Garrick had presented, and when he produced the other plays, he often restored neoclassic "improvements" that Garrick had purged.

Edmund Kean (1787–1833) brought the romantic revolution in literary taste to the Shakespearean stage. Kean's brilliant portrayals of the tragic heroes were noted for their emotional power and psychological realism, but Kean was criticized by those who preferred the older style, and his virtuoso acting tended to reduce the plays to personal vehicles—a practice that has persisted into the twentieth century.

Another nineteenth-century practice that still has proponents—especially in films—was the introduction of historical "accuracy" in costumes and staging. Although people like William Charles Macready declared that they wished to restore the plays to the versions Shakespeare wrote, they introduced a literalism to the staging that often undermined the very texts they restored. Macready restored much of Shakespeare's text to *King Lear*, even including a refined version of the Fool (whose part he assigned to a woman), but he set the play in the ancient England of Geoffrey of Monmouth's King Leir rather than the elaborately hierarchical late-medieval society with which Shakespeare's play is concerned.

Increasingly elaborate sets demanded long breaks between scenes and often required that the plays be cut and rearranged to accommodate them. And they tended to distort the plays, so that even in an age of great Shakespearean actors, general restoration of the texts, and widespread Shakespeare idolatry, Shakespeare's own theatrical genius was still obscured. In *Antony and Cleopatra*, for instance, Herbert Beerbohm Tree (1853–1917) went so far as to introduce the fabulous barge upon the stage, ignoring all the indications in the speech Shakespeare gave Enobarbus that this apotheosis of Cleopatra belonged to the Egyptian province of poetry and imagination and not to the Roman domain of visible physical reality.

Some modern productions of Shakespeare are still influenced by bad legacies from the nineteenth century: the wrongheaded devotion to literal historical accuracy, and the use of the plays as vehicles for virtuoso star performers. But the twentieth century has also brought a growing interest in recovering Shakespeare's theatrical strategies as well as his texts, and an increasing respect for his abilities as playwright as well as poet and psychologist. The pioneer in this movement was William Poel (1852–1934), who founded the Elizabethan Stage Society to stage the plays in Elizabethan style. Although Poel often cut and bowdlerized the texts, and although he did not attempt a literal reproduction of an Elizabethan playhouse, he did eliminate the elaborate scenic effects that had become traditional, as well as the footlights, complicated stage business, and virtuoso acting style of the nineteenth-century theater. Poel used no scenery at all, and he staged the plays on an open platform with a curtained inner recess and a playing space above the stage. Instead of historically "accurate" costumes, he used what Shakespeare's own actors had used— standard Elizabethan dress. Instead of footlights, he used lighting from above and in front of the stage, to reproduce the natural lighting of Shakespeare's own theater. His actors spoke their lines quickly, eliminating the stage business that had slowed performances and necessitated extensive cutting.

Poel influenced Harley Granville-Barker (1877–1946) who adapted Poel's principles to the commercial theater. Although Granville-Barker did use settings, they were suggestive rather than representational, and designed to bring out the meanings of the texts rather than compete with them. He went even further than Poel in restoring the original texts of the plays, and followed him in having the actors speak swiftly and avoid excessive stage business. Granville-Barker's productions, designed for an apron stage without footlights, were based on his sensitive studies of the texts of the plays; and his *Prefaces to Shakespeare* (1947) are still counted among the best Shakespeare criticism of the twentieth century.

Once Poel had freed the stage from the nineteenth-century tradition of historical spectacle, other directors began to experiment with new methods of staging. Perhaps the most influential of these was Sir Barry Jackson's modern-dress *Hamlet* (1925). Following Jackson, many directors have done the plays in modern dress or have transported them to a variety of post-Shake-

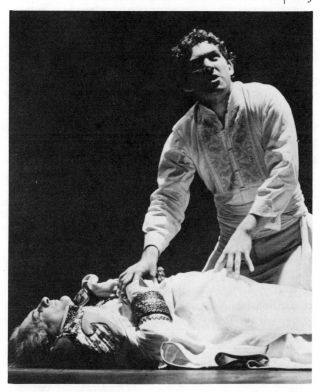

Typical of the changes in locale of many modern Shakespeare productions is this 1969 Minnesota Theatre Company *Julius Caesar* (Tyrone Guthrie Theatre, Minneapolis), set in a South American dictatorship. Here Antony (Charles Keating) mourns over the body of the slain Caesar (Robert Pastene).

THE GUTHRIE THEATER, MINNEAPOLIS

spearean settings, some of them highly effective and others merely bizarre. Orson Welles used early nineteenth-century Haiti for his "voodoo" *Macbeth* (1936) with its all-black cast, naked witch doctor, and throbbing drums. Michael Benthall's romantic, early Victorian *Hamlet* (Stratford-upon-Avon, 1948) and the

Minnesota Theater Company's *Julius Caesar*, set in a South American dictatorship (1969), are only two among many other examples.

The last fifty years, especially the years since World War II, have seen an enormous growth in popular interest in Shakespeare and a corresponding increase in Shakespeare productions all over the world. Shakespear's plays are performed by every sort of group, from amateur repertory companies to famous actors on Broadway. In England and North America various festival theaters have become a major source of Shakespeare production, and, although the history of the major festivals is as various as the history of Shakespeare production in our time, taken together, they provide impressive evidence of Shakespeare's contemporary appeal. In England, the company at Stratford-upon-Avon has grown from a small, seasonal, rural festival, turning out dull, conscientious productions, to the flourishing, year-round Royal Shakespeare Company, with a London home at the Aldwych Theatre as well as the Royal Shakespeare Theatre at Stratford; and the British National Theatre (the Old Vic's successor) now has three playhouses of its own. In the United States Joseph Papp's New York Shakespeare Festival has become the largest single arts institution in the country. And vast numbers of people who have never traveled to London or New York provide enthusiastic audiences for Shakespeare on every sort of stage, from the award-winning theater at Stratford, Ontario, to high school auditoriums in small American towns.

Stage settings today are usually fixed, simple, and unlocalized, but not always. Franco Zeffirelli designed beautiful, realistic Italian settings for his *Romeo and Juliet* (Old Vic, 1960); and, in nineteenth-century fashion, Zeffirelli cut the text and interrupted the action for the sake of the scene changes his elaborate sets required. At the opposite extreme, Michael Langham's *Hamlet* (Stratford-upon-Avon, 1956) was staged in a manner so austere that, as the *Birmingham Post* reported, Claudius had to say in the final scene " 'Set me the stoups of wine there beside me.' At Stratford he cannot say 'upon the table' because there is no table."

For a time it had seemed that Poel and Granville-Barker would set the course for twentieth-century Shakespeare production. But the tradition they sought to recover of uncut Elizabethan-style productions has given way to a new rage for "improving" and modernizing the plays. Not content with devising new settings, modern producers have cut, augmented, rearranged, and rewritten Shakespeare's plays, sometimes to brilliant effect, sometimes disastrously. Variety and innovation, along with an effort to discover contemporary relevance in the plays, have become the dominant characteristics of Shakespeare production in our time. Orson Welles was not the only director to discover an anticipation of twentieth-century fascism in *Julius Caesar* or Paul Robeson the only actor to discover an anticipation of modern American racism in Othello. Modernization, in fact, has become an important new tradition.

Unrestrained innovation has sometimes degenerated into eccentricity, as in Joseph Papp's zany, contemporary *Hamlet* (Public Theater, 1968). Papp's Hamlet gave Claudius an exploding cigar, sold peanuts and balloons to the audience, and delivered his soliloquies in a variety of bizarre styles, ranging from a Puerto Rican accent to an imitation of a ventriloquist's dummy (for this, he sat on the ghost's lap). Papp's Ophelia was a sexy blonde in a miniskirt, who sang, like a nightclub entertainer, through a hand microphone, and Papp's version of the duel between Hamlet and Laertes was a game of Russian roulette. On the whole, however, Papp's enterprises have had better success, attracting large, heterogeneous audiences with contemporary productions, relevant to their own experience and unencumbered by conventional pieties.

The modern theater has had its share of great Shakespearean performers—artists like John Gielgud, Laurence Olivier, and Edith Evans could probably stand with the greatest of their predecessors—but the real star of a contemporary Shakespeare production is most likely to be a virtuoso producer-director who shapes every aspect of it to fit his own conception. Peter Brook illustrates both the best and the worst of this new tradition. Brook's *Titus Andronicus* (Stratford-upon-Avon, 1955) has been called the greatest Shakespeare production of our time. Inspired by Antonin Artaud's demand for a theater that would function as sacrificial rite, Brook discovered beneath the clumsy poetry and mechanical plot of Shakespeare's earliest tragedy a reincarnation of primeval terror and an anticipation of the contemporary theater of cruelty. Brook's Titus was Laurence Olivier, and Olivier gave one of his greatest performances. But the production (for which Brook wrote the music and designed the costumes and scenery, as well as doing the directing) is always identified as Brook's *Titus Andronicus*, not Olivier's. Brook's *King Lear* (Stratford-upon-Avon, 1962), although even better known than his *Titus Andronicus*, was less illuminating. Like his *Titus Andronicus*, Brook's *King Lear* was an unrelenting vision of horror, but in this case the vision seemed inadequate to Shakespeare's play. Brook ruthlessly cut every manifestation of human goodness and compassion, reducing Shakespeare's monumental tragedy of faith and despair to an expression of despair, pure and simple (or, in the words of a Stratford brochure, "lucid and Brechtian").

All these efforts to modernize Shakespeare and to find new meaning in his text—sometimes to work deliberately against the text in the interest of a directorial theory or obsession—have drawn outraged protests from Shakespeareans. And yet the tradition of improving and modernizing Shakespeare is almost as old as the plays themselves, dating as it does from the days of Davenant. In fact, Shakespeare was a great improver and modernizer, adapting his sources and dressing his actors to suit his own conceptions and the fashions of his own time.

If modern improvements sometimes obscure Shakespeare's art, they also demonstrate its continuing vitality and its capacity to reveal new dimensions of significance to successive ages and audiences. The nineteenth-century sensibility seemed uniquely qualified to appreciate the psychological subtleties of Hamlet's character, and the existential horror of Lear's story seems to reveal itself today as never before. To be sure, nineteenth-century interpretations have been criticized in our time for overemphasizing the prince at the expense of the play and forgetting that Shakespeare's title is not simply *Hamlet* but *Hamlet, Prince of Denmark*, and future critics will undoubtedly find distortions to correct in our own passionately contemporary readings of *King Lear*. All productions, even the most faithful, are necessarily interpretations; and all interpretations, whether implicitly suggested on stage or explicitly laid out in program notes or critical essays, are necessarily partial. Olivier may have distorted Shakespeare's *Hamlet* with his Freudian interpretation, but he also revealed new aspects of its greatness; and although Peter Brook left out much of Shakespeare's *King Lear* by interpreting it as an early version of Samuel Beckett's *Endgame*, he also showed us a side of it that no sentimental production or optimistic interpretation could ever convey.

Brook has been deeply influenced by Jan Kott, and like Kott he has been criticized for playing fast and loose with Shakespeare's meanings. But the title of

Kott's brilliant, eccentric book of Shakespeare criticism is *Shakespeare Our Contemporary*, and if these tragedies are to retain the vitality they have had for the past four hundred years we will need people like Brook and Kott who see them as mirrors to our own deepest concerns and not simply as windows to well-preserved antiquity. In this very important sense, some of the most radical innovators have been most faithful to the spirit of Shakespeare's art.

NOTES

Chronology

1. All Shakespeare quotations are taken from *The Complete Plays and Poems of William Shakespeare* (New Cambridge Edition), ed. William Allan Neilson and Charles Jarvis Hill (Boston, Houghton Mifflin, 1942). Readers using other editions will notice slight differences in language and punctuation.

The Tragedies

1. See especially Robert Penn Warren's famous and often reprinted essay, "Pure and Impure Poetry," which originally appeared in *The Kenyon Review*, Spring, 1943, pp. 228–54.

2. This phrase from a sixteenth-century sermon by Henry Bullinger—*The Decades of Henry Bullinger*, translated by H. I., ed. Thomas Harding (Cambridge, Parker Society, 1849–1852), Vol. I, p. 205—expresses the standard view. Compare C. S. Lewis, *Studies in Words* (Cambridge, Cambridge University Press, 1960), p. 54, in which Lewis glosses the word "Nature" in *2 Henry IV*, IV, v, 66, as follows: "The choice of the word *nature*, in the context, would in Shake-

speare's time have made the theological implication clear. *Nature* means 'we human beings in our natural condition,' that is, unless or until touched by grace."

3. Noted by R. A. Foakes in "An Approach to *Julius Caesar*," *Shakespeare Quarterly*, Summer, 1954, pp. 267–68.

4. One of the best Aristotelian analyses of the plot of *Hamlet* is Francis Fergusson's in *The Idea of a Theater* (Princeton, Princeton University Press, 1949). Aristotle defines the "reversal" (*Poetics*, ch. X–XI, translated by S. H. Butcher, 4th ed., New York, Dover, 1951) as a "change by which the action veers round to its opposite" and the "recognition" as a "change from ignorance to knowledge." "The best form of recognition," he says, "is coincident with" a reversal, and both "should arise from the internal structure of the plot, so that what follows should be the necessary or probable result of the preceding action."

5. My discussion of the play within the play is greatly indebted to Maynard Mack's brilliant essay "The World of *Hamlet*," *The Yale Review*, June, 1952, pp. 502–23.

6. Lewes Lavater, *Of Ghosts and Spirits Walking by Night*, translated by R. H. (London, 1587), reprinted in the Norton Critical Edition of *Hamlet*, ed. Cyrus Hoy (New York, Norton, 1963), p. 111. Lavater does concede, however, that both good and evil angels sometimes appear in various shapes to people on earth.

7. The Folio reads "solid," but many modern editors give "sullied," following the Quarto version "sallied," which is a sixteenth-century form of "sullied."

8. For a sensitive essay on the significance of the language and imagery in *Othello*, see G. Wilson Knight's "The *Othello* Music" in his *The Wheel of Fire*, rev. ed. (London, Methuen, 1949).

9. Some editors, following the Folio reading, give "Judean" instead of "Indian." The exact meaning of the allusion, whether the word is "Judean" or "Indian," has been the subject of considerable scholarly debate.

10. A. C. Bradley, *Shakespearean Tragedy* (Cleveland,

World, 1955), pp. 233–34 (first ed.: London, Macmillan, 1904).

11. J. Stampfer, "The Catharsis of *King Lear*," *Shakespeare Survey*, 13, 1960, pp. 1–10.

12. Harold C. Goddard, *The Meaning of Shakespeare* (Chicago, University of Chicago Press, 1951), Vol. II, p. 170.

13. Although some critics have seen Coriolanus as a noble tragic hero, many others have adopted Oscar James Campbell's view that the play is really a satire and Coriolanus the object of Shakespeare's scorn and ridicule. See Campbell's *Shakespeare's Satire* (New York, Oxford University Press, 1943), pp. 198–216.

14. Plutarch's *Life of Martius Coriolanus*, translated by Sir Thomas North. Good modern editions are *Shakespeare's Plutarch*, ed. Walter W. Skeat (London, Macmillan, 1875) and *Shakespeare's Plutarch*, ed. T. J. B. Spencer (London, Penguin, 1964).

15. *Vir* does not have the same ambiguity as English "man," which sometimes means "man" as opposed to "woman" and sometimes "human" as opposed to "beast." In Latin another word, *homo*, expressed the generic concept "human."

Shakespeare's Tragedies on Stage

1. But since the staging was conventional and symbolic rather than realistic, he did not always have to do so. See Bernard Beckerman, *Shakespeare at the Globe* (New York, Macmillan, 1962), pp. 183–92, for good arguments that he did not.

BIBLIOGRAPHY

Editions: A Selection

MULTI-VOLUME EDITIONS

Furness, H. H., et. al., *A New Variorum Edition of Shakespeare*, Philadelphia, Lippincott (and successors), 1871–present. Each volume annotated with copious selections from the commentators and variant readings, as well as material on the sources, evidence for the date, and so forth. This edition provides the fullest material for detailed study of the plays.

Ellis-Fermor, Una, H. F. Brooks, H. Jenkins, et. al., *The Arden Shakespeare*, London, Methuen, 1951–present. These are revised versions of the Arden editions, which were founded in 1890 and edited by W. J. Craig and R. H. Case. Like the *Variorum*, a useful edition, one volume to a play. Each contains stimulating introductory discussions of the critical and textual problems as well as useful annotations of the text and selections from the sources.

Harbage, Alfred, general editor, *The Pelican Shakespeare*, Baltimore, Penguin, 1956–67. These are good, inexpensive paperback editions of the individual plays with introductions by various distinguished editors.

ONE-VOLUME EDITIONS

Neilson, William Allan, and Charles Jarvis Hill, *The Complete Plays and Poems of William Shakespeare*, Boston, Houghton Mifflin, 1942. This is probably the best of the older one-volume editions.

Harbage, Alfred, general editor, *William Shakespeare: The Complete Works*, Baltimore, Penguin, 1969. This is a revised one-volume version of *The Pelican Shakespeare*. The introductory material here, by various editors, is fuller than in the Neilson and Hill edition.

Evans, G. Blakemore, et. al., *The Riverside Shakespeare*, Boston, Houghton Mifflin, 1974. This edition is especially valuable for its completely reedited text and for its appendixes on stage history and on early references to Shakespeare and his works.

Secondary Sources: An Introductory Guide

BACKGROUND MATERIAL

Chute, Marchette, *Shakespeare of London*, New York, Dutton, 1949.

Halliday, F. E., *A Shakespeare Companion 1564–1964*, Baltimore, Penguin, 1964.

Harrison, G. B., *Introducing Shakespeare*, Baltimore, Penguin, 1954.

Kökeritz, Helge, *Shakespeare's Pronunciation*, New Haven, Conn., Yale University Press, 1953.

Spencer, T. J. B., ed., *Shakespeare's Plutarch*, Baltimore, Penguin, 1964.

Tillyard, E. M. W., *The Elizabethan World Picture*, New York, Random House, 1961.

Wilson, John Dover, *Life in Shakespeare's England*, Baltimore, Penguin, 1944.

DISCUSSIONS OF THE PLAYS

Bevington, David, ed., *Twentieth Century Interpretations of Hamlet*, Englewood Cliffs, N.J., Prentice-Hall, 1968. See also other volumes in this series, on other plays.

Bradley, A. C., *Shakespearean Tragedy*, Cleveland, Meridian, 1955 (originally published by Macmillan in 1904).

Burckhardt, Sigurd, *Shakespearean Meanings*, Princeton, N.J., Princeton University Press, 1968.

Calderwood, James L., and Harold E. Toliver, eds., *Essays in Shakespearean Criticism*, Englewood Cliffs, N.J., Prentice-Hall, 1970.

Charney, Maurice, ed., *Discussions of Shakespeare's Roman Plays*, Boston, D. C. Heath, 1964. See also other volumes in this series.

Dean, Leonard, ed., *Shakespeare: Modern Essays in Criticism*, rev. ed., New York, Oxford University Press, 1967. Like Calderwood and Toliver's and Kernan's, Dean's book is a useful paperback anthology of essays on the various plays by distinguished critics.

Goddard, Harold C., *The Meaning of Shakespeare*, Chicago, University of Chicago Press, 1951. A separate essay for each play.

Granville-Barker, Harley, *Prefaces to Shakespeare*, Princeton, N.J., Princeton University Press, 1946–47.

Kernan, Alvin B., ed., *Modern Shakespearean Criticism*, New York, Harcourt, Brace, 1970.

Knight, G. Wilson, *The Wheel of Fire: Interpretations of Shakespearean Tragedy*, New York, Meridian, 1957.

Kott, Jan, *Shakespeare Our Contemporary*, Garden City, N.Y., Doubleday, 1966.

Lerner, Laurence, ed., *Shakespeare's Tragedies: An Anthology of Modern Criticism*, Baltimore, Penguin, 1963.

Mack, Maynard, *King Lear in Our Time*, Berkeley, University of California Press, 1965.

Siegel, Paul N., *Shakespearean Tragedy and the Eliza-
    bethan Compromise*, New York, New York Uni-
    versity Press, 1957.
Speaight, Robert, *Nature in Shakespearean Tragedy*,
    New York, Macmillan, 1962.

INDEX